One Step at a Time

And Other Devotions for Teachers

HESTER MONSMA

Baker Book House
Grand Rapids, Michigan 49506

Copyright 1984 by
Baker Book House Company

ISBN: 0-8010-6177-6

First printing, September 1984
Second printing, August 1985

Printed in the United States of America

Scripture references are from the Holy Bible: New International Version,
copyright © 1978 by the International Bible Society.

To my first and best teacher,

my mother,

Marie Vos Monsma

Contents

1
One Step at a Time

Suggested Bible Reading: Matthew 6:25–34

Do not be anxious about anything, but in everything, by prayer and petition, with thanksgiving, present your requests to God. And the peace of God, which transcends all understanding, will guard your hearts and your minds in Christ Jesus [Phil. 4:6–7].

The pensive look in the eyes of the five-year-old that summer day showed that something was troubling him. "What's the matter, Marty? What are you thinking about?" I asked.

"I'm thinking about school."

"Good! I hope they're happy thoughts."

"Not really. . . . I guess I'm sort of scared."

"But why?" I persisted.

"Well, I'm really not so scared about kindergarten. I think I can do that, and maybe even first grade won't be so bad. But then it will keep getting harder and harder. There's going to be junior high, then high school, and finally I'll have to go to college and that will be the worst of all!"

So I tried to allay his apprehension, explaining to him that as he grew older and bigger God would also make his mind grow, so that college at age eighteen should be no more difficult for him than kindergarten at age five.

Whether I succeeded in calming his fears that day, I really don't know. But I do know that in the years since then I've often had opportunity to remind myself of the same truth, even though in slightly different form.

When a task has looked overwhelming or when fears cloud an unknown future, I've reminded myself, "But you don't have to conquer it all at once; you don't have to have all the answers right now. The same God who helps a five-year-old develop, both mentally and physically, so that he's ready to face life's tasks as he matures, will be with you as you meet new challenges, as you are given difficult problems to solve, or as you face an unknown future."

Thank you, God, for the assurance that you are always with me, in troubled times as well as in happy times. May I rely completely on you for all I need, knowing that you will be with me in the future as you have been in the past, and experiencing that those who put their trust in you will never be disappointed. May God's peace always be very real to me. In Jesus' name, Amen.

2
Discover God's World

Suggested Bible Reading: Psalm 8

When I consider your heavens,
  the work of your fingers,
the moon and the stars,
  which you have set in place,
what is man that you are mindful of him,
  the son of man that you care for him?   [Ps. 8:3–4]

Today was the first day of school . . . halls filled with children wondering who their teacher will be and whether their best friend will be in their room . . . parents accompanying many of the younger children, seeing them safely settled in their classroom. Teachers too, eager, wondering what their new class will be like, with even the most experienced admitting they did not sleep as well as usual, and all feeling a bit of apprehension at the start of another year.

As I walk down the hall I am impressed by the display case one of our teachers has prepared and I can't help but think how fitting it is for the beginning of school. "Discover God's World" is lettered in the background. Attractively arranged are various items from God's creation: an insect collection, cattails, a wasp nest. I am pleased when I notice some of the students stop to examine it and I hope it will motivate them to happily "Discover God's World" this school year—not only in the field of science, but also in social studies, music, literature, math, and whatever else the teachers will be presenting to them. I hope parents will also take notice of it and will reinforce at home what we are doing in school.

I trust that this year students and teachers will not be afraid to tackle unknown subjects, to try new approaches, and to attempt what has not been attempted before in their quest to "Discover God's World."

Whenever we are tempted to continue on and on in the same way it is good to remind ourselves of the foolish cat in the nursery rhyme:

"Pussy cat, pussy cat, where have you been?"
"I've been to London to visit the queen."
"Pussy cat, pussy cat, what did you there?"
"I frightened a little mouse under her chair!"

Can you imagine being so fortunate that you are granted an audience with the queen? How we would prepare for it, and how we would look forward to it. And yet what does the cat of our nursery rhyme do? Chases mice . . . something he could just as well do in anybody's barn or garage! What a wasted opportunity!

Yet isn't it easy for us to slip into the same old patterns? It's much less time-consuming to use last year's test than to construct a new one; it's more comfortable to teach that particular unit in exactly the same way we did last year and the year before than to revise and rework it. But if we continue on the same way, simply because it's easier, if we fail to take advantage of new opportunities as they are presented to us, we are not that much different from the students who are content to learn as little as they can and who pass up many opportunities to expand their knowledge and benefit from new experiences.

May we as teachers accept the challenge to "Discover God's World" and in doing this for ourselves may we open the way for our students to do the same. Let us never be content simply to "chase mice" when so many glorious opportunities await us!

We pray, Lord, that you will help all of us—parents, teachers, and students—to widen our horizons and to take advantage of every opportunity to learn and to discover what you have given us. May we continually seek new ways to learn more about your world and to pass this on to our students in the classroom. In Christ, Amen.

3
Doors

Suggested Bible Reading: Philippians 4:10–20

. . . for I have learned to be content whatever the circumstances [Phil. 4:11].

His parents lived only one house away from school and he, their youngest son, had spent many an hour with his friends on the school playground. He eagerly looked forward to the day when he too would start school. Surely there would not be an adjustment problem for him when September rolled around!

The first day of school his mother accompanied him and saw to it that he arrived safely at the kindergarten room. He came home later in the day, happy and enthusiastic, eager to tell his family about his experiences. But the next morning when it was time for Keith to leave for school, his mother was surprised when he insisted that she bring him as far as the school door: "Not to my room, but just come along until I'm in school." As she walked the short distance with him she probed gently, trying to discover what might be the reason for this surprising request. But all to no avail.

When he repeated this request the next day, his parents confronted him directly: "Why can't you walk to school by yourself?" He refused to give a reason other than "I just want you to walk with me."

Not until a week later, when his parents firmly told him, "We will not walk with you to school anymore," did the truth come out as he burst into tears. "But what if I can't get the school door open?"

Who knows how many of the students you face every day have doors they fear they may not be able to open. Literal doors, yes . . . but much more frightening to a developing youngster, figurative doors: the doors of making friends, of doing well on a crucial test, of making the

11

soccer team, of being chosen for the class play, of understanding that new math concept. The list could go on and on.

Granted, there are going to be closed doors which our students will meet and which will probably never open for them, just as you and I have experienced closed doors in our lives. Yet as teachers it is our responsibility to be tuned in to the fears our students may have about closed doors, to help them open doors if we feel they should be opened, and to help them accept graciously and willingly any doors which may remain closed to them. It is well that both adults and children learn to say with the apostle Paul, "For I have learned to be content whatever the circumstances."

Dear Lord, help me to accept whatever you plan for my life — closed doors as well as opened doors. May I also be sensitive to my students' needs and the closed doors with which they may meet. Give me the ability to help them open closed doors if such is your will or accept thankfully and graciously any doors which remain closed to them. For Jesus' sake, Amen.

4
First or Last?

Suggested Bible Reading: Mark 9:33–37

Sitting down, Jesus called the Twelve and said, "If anyone wants to be first, he must be the very last . . ." [Mark 9:35].

Those kids won't let me play with them," were the words with which a third grader approached me as I was taking my turn at playground duty. "Those kids" were some of his classmates who were busily involved in a game of tetherball.

So the two of us walked over and I inquired why Curt wasn't allowed to join them. "He may play with us . . . we don't care," was the response.

"See, Curt, it's all set. Go ahead and have a good time together," I said and then wandered off to another section of the playground to see how things were going there.

Ten minutes later I was back near the tetherball site, but noticed that Curt was nowhere to be seen. Glancing around, I soon spied him sitting on the cement, leaning disconsolately against the brick wall of the school. "What happened, boys?" I asked. "I thought you said Curt might play with you."

"We did, but he wouldn't go to the end of the line like he's supposed to. He never wants to take turns," they added, "but always thinks he has to be first." Small wonder, I thought, that Curt has trouble making friends and is often seen alone on the playground.

But then my thoughts continued—how easy to condemn a third grader for his unwillingness to "take turns." Yet often aren't we adults guilty of the same thing? It's sometimes hard for us to relinquish first place to someone else, to step into the background so that others may go before us. When we ask God for something we seem to expect an answer right now and if God's response is,

13

"Wait a while," it's so easy to become discouraged and impatient.

May God give us the grace to be willing to wait, to be willing to be last, and to remember the words of Christ when he said, "If anyone wants to be first, he must be the very last."

Lord, forgive my impatience and my striving to be first. May I be willing to be a servant so that your kingdom may be furthered and your name glorified. Help me to teach this lesson to my students also. In Jesus' name I pray, Amen.

5
New Days

Suggested Bible Reading: Isaiah 65:17–25

The former things will not be remembered. . . [Isa. 65:17].

I'm sure you all know the kind of day I'm thinking of — the kind when nothing seems to go right. It begins when you step out of the car at school and a batch of papers that you had marked so carefully the night before slips out of your arms. Fortunately there's no wind or mud puddles, so you quickly retrieve them and hurry on into school, eager to put the finishing touches on your plans for the day. But you're hardly in your room when the secretary calls you to the phone and you spend ten precious minutes explaining to a parent why it was necessary for Sue to redo her math paper, and why you insisted that this be done before she came to school. The conversation ends on an amiable note and you rush to use the ditto machine only to find three teachers ahead of you. When it's finally your turn, the machine has run out of ditto fluid and the bell's due to ring in two minutes.

"I'll ask my aide to run these off," you think, only to return to your room to find a note on your desk informing you that she is sick and will not be in.

So the day continues: the bulb on the slide projector burns out just as you are ready to show a filmstrip; one of the students is nauseated at her desk; the principal comes in to observe your math class just as you're trying to decide what to do in lieu of handing out the papers you had intended to have duplicated; an announcement warning students to stay off the neighbor's lawn interrupts you just when you have students spellbound in your recounting of the story of Paul Revere's ride. You finally breathe a sigh of relief as the day comes to an end, only to find, as you sink exhausted into the chair behind your desk, that the newsletters you were supposed to send home with the students are still neatly stacked in front of you.

But you brace yourself with the thought, "Tomorrow is another day and I know it's going to be better . . . I'll run those papers off on the ditto machine before I go home tonight; I'll distribute the newsletters the first thing in the morning; I'll remind students again that if they feel sick they should quickly leave the room without waiting for special permission to do so."

It's a good feeling, as we look back on a day when things did not run smoothly, that we may look forward to a better day tomorrow. But this is true to an even greater extent when we look back at our sins of the past day. We know that not only is there forgiveness from God if we repent and ask for it, but also each new day is a gift from him. I often think that our lives are like a book, with each page a pure white blank. We soil and smudge the page as we go through the day, but every morning — by God's grace — we turn to a new page, sparkling clean and white . . . leaving the old, dirty page behind. How thankful we should be for a new page each day and for God's promise that "the former things will not be remembered."

> Thank you, Lord, for your promise not to remember my sins and failures. Thank you for new opportunities every day, both in my personal life and in my dealings with my students. Help me, then, to make the most of each day and to thank you continually for all your mercies toward me. For Jesus' sake, Amen.

6
Memory Work

Suggested Bible Reading: Psalm 119:97– 112

*Your word is a lamp to my feet
and a light for my path*   [Ps. 119:105].

If you are a teacher in a Christian school, or perhaps a Sunday-school teacher, I hope you still require your students to memorize Bible passages and individual texts. Granted, it may not be the most exciting part of the day for the students, and it will require determination and persistence on your part, but chances are great that sooner or later in life the words boys and girls memorized while under your supervision will be very precious to them.

The husband of a close friend of mine had been involved in an automobile accident and as a result could not work for an extended period of time. Reading and any type of concentration were difficult for him. She wrote, "We find that the best therapy for Don is just to take long walks together. As we do this we often recite Bible verses we have learned earlier in life. It's surprising how many we can recall and what a comfort they are to us."

How often, as a person finds himself in circumstances when he is not able to read, he still receives great comfort from God's Word by recalling passages which had been memorized earlier. People suffering on beds of illness, perhaps even too weak to hold a Bible, servicemen or women in faraway places, a lonely student away from home for the first time — all have testified as to the comfort and strength these gems from the Bible have given them.

As teachers let us also set an example for our students by continuing the practice of memorizing Bible passages. Let them know we do this, and let them see how important it is to us.

If students can sense our enthusiasm and can begin to understand the comfort that memorized Bible passages have brought to others, memorization need not be treated as a difficult-to-motivate part of the day. Yes, "Thy Word have I hid in my heart." Do you make it a daily practice to hide God's Word in your heart? Is it your desire that your students also are motivated to do this?

Thank you, Father in heaven, for the ability to memorize. May we be able to give our students the desire to lay up God's Word in their hearts and may we ourselves set an example for them in this. In Christ's name, Amen.

7
Spend It Wisely

Suggested Bible Reading: Ephesians 5:8 – 21

Be very careful, then, how you live — not as unwise but as wise, making the most of every opportunity, because the days are evil [Eph. 5:15].

The other day, while going through one of my drawers, I came across a letter written several years ago and addressed to me. It was from one of my nieces who lived thousands of miles away and who must have been about eight years old at the time. Taped very carefully across the top of the paper, so that Lincoln's head was in an upright position on every one of them, were five pennies. The letter bore reference to these: "As you see, I put five cents on the top of the page and I would like you to spend them very wisely because this is all the money I have. Now I do not have any money left at all."

"The widow's mite," I remember thinking at the time. I also recall her mother writing to me, "This was her own idea and it really is all the money she has. The pennies are filled with as much love as Judy could send."

Undoubtedly the admonition to "spend it wisely" was one she had often heard from her parents, for saving money and spending it wisely somehow were more difficult for her than for her brothers and sisters. So now she dutifully passed this bit of wisdom on to her aunt!

It is good for all of us to be reminded to spend our money wisely, but it is just as important that we spend wisely another commodity God has given us — our time. I can almost hear God paraphrasing Judy's advice: "I have given you sixty minutes every hour. I want you to spend them wisely because when those sixty minutes are spent they are gone forever. I cannot give those minutes to you again because they simply do not exist anymore."

Time, both in the classroom and out of it, must be

19

spent wisely. I have yet to meet a teacher who claimed to have enough time to do everything she would like to do in any given day. So, with time at a premium, how important it is that we spend it wisely. We owe it to our students, to their parents, to the board that employs us, and to our God to spend wisely every minute that the students are under our tutelage.

Also, outside of school hours, our time is not ours, but God's. We must plan wisely so that we have adequate time to prepare the next week's lessons, to mark conscientiously the papers handed in that day, and to contribute constructively to school-related committees on which we have been asked to serve. But we must also budget our time so that our family is not neglected, so that we can serve, at least to a limited extent, our church and community, and so that we have time to unwind and relax. Quite an order, with only so many hours in a day, but one worth striving for — also asking God for help in our quest for allocating our time in a responsible way.

I don't know if I'll ever spend Judy's five pennies — as yet the pack rat in me hasn't allowed it! Perhaps I'll just keep them as a reminder to myself of how an eight-year-old taught me an important lesson: that not only money, but also another gift of God — that of the priceless commodity called time — must be spent wisely.

We are grateful, Lord, for the many gifts you give to us. Help us to be wise stewards of not only our money, but also our time. May we avoid the extremes of wasting hour after hour in nonproductive, selfish interests; may we also avoid the error of never taking time to relax and enjoy the blessings of life you have given us in family and friends, in the world of nature, and in other interests we may have. In the classroom, too, may I use the time wisely . . . realizing that it is not only my time that I'm responsible for, but also the time of every student in my class. In Jesus' name, Amen.

8
Wolf!

Suggested Bible Reading: Proverbs 13:1– 15

He who guards his lips guards his life,
  but he who speaks rashly will come to ruin [Prov. 13:3].

One important bit of advice often given to beginning teachers is the reminder, "Be sure you are consistent and follow through on what you say."

"Do not make threats or promises which you will be unable or unwilling to enforce" is the way one teacher's handbook expresses this principle. I hope none of you has ever been put in the position of the teacher who told his class, "No one is going to leave for home until I find out who threw that pencil across the room!" No one admitted it, the school buses had to leave, and the teacher had an important committee meeting thirty minutes after school was dismissed. You can imagine what the pupils' reaction was the next time he threatened them with punishment.

We all know the story of the boy who falsely cried "Wolf!" so often that when he actually did see one and tried to warn others, they did not believe him. This reminds me of an experience I had recently. I was attending a convention and it was near the supper hour. Suddenly a loud clanging was heard throughout the dormitory where we were staying. Stepping out into the hall, we could see the word *fire* flashing on and off by the fire extinguishers. Slightly amused, because it all seemed so innocent, we milled around in the halls until school personnel came and told us, "Everyone must go outdoors!" So we complied, soon to be told it was a false alarm and we could go back to our rooms.

The next evening the same thing happened and, remembering the false alarm of the night before, the two of us who were still dressed did leave the room and go to the central area, while our two suitemates, who were ready to retire, calmly remained in the room.

This time various explanations were given: the overly sensitive smoke detectors in each dorm room were reacting to the high humidity . . . a person smoking too near the smoke detector was triggering it. At any rate, when the clanging started again at six o'clock the next morning none of us made any effort to leave the room, but turned over in our beds for another hour's sleep. We were just like those who heard the boy cry "Wolf!" and — could it be — like our students who soon learn whether our warnings or requests mean anything or not.

How thankful we should be that we have a God who gives no false alarms, who never cries "Wolf!" unless there is danger present. Have you ever thought how difficult our lives would be if our God would go back on his Word, if he didn't mean exactly what he tells us in the Bible? True, there were times when he had to punish those he loved (and perhaps we will too): patient, long-suffering Moses was not allowed to enter the Promised Land because he struck the rock instead of speaking to it; David's son had to die even though God had completely forgiven David for his sin with Bathsheba.

Do your students see you as one who speaks carefully and acts consistently . . . who never gives false alarms or cries "Wolf!" unnecessarily? Do they view you as one who has fair rules, which you insist must be followed and obeyed? To be an effective teacher, this certainly is necessary. God grant that you may fulfill this requirement.

> Help me, Lord, to be consistent in what I do and say. May I never say things I don't mean or make threats or promises I cannot enforce. Forgive me if I do these things and help me to be a more effective teacher because students, parents, and coworkers view me as a person who speaks carefully and who acts consistently. In his name, Amen.

9
Appearances

Suggested Bible Reading: 1 Samuel 16:1– 13

But the LORD said to Samuel, "Do not consider his appearance or his height, for I have rejected him. The LORD does not look at the things man looks at. Man looks at the outward appearance, but the LORD looks at the heart " [1 Sam. 16:7].

I know all conscientious educators desire to give every student an equal chance and want to be fair to all of them. Yet studies show that attractive children receive better grades than unattractive children, that they receive more attention and more praise, are chosen more often, and have greater expectations placed upon them than those not as attractive. All of this is certainly going to result in a better self-image and consequently a better chance at success. It also leads me to ask, "Are we judging our students merely by what we see on the outside, or by what God sees . . . what is in the heart?"

A few years ago, when my brother was a missionary in Nigeria, I visited him and his family. One of the first things I noticed was the mottoes painted on the front of every truck or lorry. "Glory Be to God," "Love and Peace," "God Will Provide," "God First," "O Lord I Promise," "The Lord Is My Shepherd," "By the Grace of God," "Trust in God," "Save Me O God" are but a few of the eighty-some mottoes I jotted down as we traveled the highways. At least 90 percent of these had religious overtones. (We did, however, get a chuckle out of the pragmatist who proclaimed to all who saw his lorry "No Money, No Friend" and felt pity for the owner who could think of nothing better than "African Saloon" for his motto!)

When I remarked that there certainly seemed to be a multitude of Christian owners of lorries, my brother responded that this was not necessarily the case. "For some of the drivers," Tim continued, "it may really mean something and be a reflection of the owner's beliefs. But in many cases, perhaps most of them, it's just the thing to do and the words have no real significance for them."

"So here's another case of what one sees on the outside not portraying accurately what is on the inside," I found myself thinking.

I sincerely hope that people with whom you work and fellowship will readily see that you are a child of God. I also hope that this will be an accurate portrayal of the love of Christ and the desire to do his will which is lodged deep in your heart.

If you as a teacher have this love for Christ deep within you, and if you are consistently conscious of looking beyond a student's features, if you can ignore an unbecoming hair style or an unattractive manner of dress, then you will be on the road to following God's example when he told Samuel, "Man looks at the outward appearance, but the Lord looks at the heart." By looking at the heart and character of a student you will be doing what God expects of you. Then your Christianity will be more than empty slogans and pious phrases, as was the case with so many Nigerian lorry owners!

Dear God, help my life to be more than one of paying attention only to the externals. Although I realize these must not be ignored, may I never forget that what is in the heart is the all-important ingredient in a person's life. May I never forget your message to Samuel. For Christ's sake, Amen.

10
Values

Suggested Bible Reading: Matthew 6:19–34

"Do not store up for yourselves treasures on earth, where moth and rust destroy, and where thieves break in and steal. But store up for yourselves treasures in heaven, where moth and rust do not destroy, and where thieves do not break in and steal. For where your treasure is, there your heart will be also." [Matt. 6:19–21].

When I was a counselor at a summer camp several years ago, one of our favorite Sunday afternoon pastimes was to walk to a nearby cemetery and examine the tombstones. It was an old cemetery, no longer used, and some of the markers dated back to a hundred years ago. Pushing away the tangle of grasses and weeds and then deciphering the well-worn headstones was an experience new to most of the young campers and one which was equally intriguing to them.

They were surprised at the number of young children buried there and were particularly impressed by a couple of families who had lost several children within a span of one or two years.

That evening in our devotions together, for this was a Christian camp, I frequently would refer to our visit earlier in the day. We would discuss the many children—often the campers' own ages—who were buried there.

Then I would try to guide the discussion to what we consider important in this life. Campers admitted that very often the most important things to them were belonging to the "in" group, having the latest style in clothes, making the basketball team or cheerleading squad, having lots of friends, having money, or "being smart." My next remark would be, "Remember the tombstone we saw of that twelve-year-old girl? If she had all those things we just mentioned, which of them is doing her any good now?"

25

The answer was obvious and so was my next question: "What is the only thing in the life of that girl that makes a difference right now?" The answer was readily given: "Whether she was a Christian or not . . . whether she's in heaven now or not." I am sure the point was driven home to the campers and I hope the lesson was not forgotten. After all, values in life are extremely important.

That reminds me of some of the subtle ways we may be instilling values in our students' lives. We compliment them on the new outfit they are wearing or on their new hairdo. We tell them that was a neat performance on the soccer field the night before. We give them credit for earning first chair in band or for doing very well on a test. All of these perhaps deserve mention, but often they are not real demonstrations of character and the Christian qualities we so desire to see in our students.

I would hope that teachers also remember to commend students for other traits they show: "That was considerate of you when you helped Sue find her lost book." "Thank you for asking Tom to join you in your softball game." "I understand you're a big help to your parents at home. That's great!" Remember that it is by example we teach, and by watching us that our students learn.

> Grant, Lord, that I may be able to instill in my students the Christian values that are all-important. May I not be guilty of emphasizing the transient and the material to the exclusion of lasting values. Help me, then, as I attempt to show by word and by deed what the important things in life really are. For Christ's sake, Amen.

11
Training

Suggested Bible Reading: Proverbs 22:1 – 16

Train a child in the way he should go,
and when he is old he will not turn from it [Prov.
22:6].

There are three phases to the training," our instructor
told us. "These are focus, communication, and dominance. *Focus* means you must have the pupil's attention
at all times. *Communication* is equally important — this is
usually done verbally, by speaking; it can also be done
silently, by sign language; and it is done by making cor-
rections when wrong actions are taken. Finally is *dominance*. You must be in control and the student must know
this. When you have accomplished all three, the training
will be complete."

Does it sound a little as if you're back in a college
classroom and the professor is giving an introductory lecture about how to be an effective teacher? You're right
that it's an introductory lecture in a class, but here the
similarity ends, for this was the opening session in an
obedience class for dogs. The class is composed of only
four students: Benny, an overweight black Lab that the
instructor insists must lose several pounds; Sandy, my
golden retriever, a gift to me from our students a year
ago; Shoshe, an alert, friendly Akita whose tail is always
tightly curled to form a complete circle; and Taffy ("Taffy
the Pistol" our instructor calls her), a nine-month-old,
active, apricot-colored poodle that is clearly in control of
her mistress at this point . . . we'll see if her owner ever
reaches the "dominance" stage with her!

So we were introduced to the world of "heel," "sit,"
"stay," "down," and "no!" It remains to be seen
whether, after six weeks of training, our dogs will be
models of canine decorum and behavior. Clearly more

27

depends on us as trainers than on the dogs themselves!

As the instructor was speaking and demonstrating, I could not help but notice the many similarities between the training of one of God's species of animals and the training of the children he has placed in our classrooms. *Focus* — yes, it's essential we have the attention of our students whenever we are speaking. *Communication* — done by speaking and writing, but there are other ways also: a look of approval or disapproval, a shake of the head, a smile, a pointing of the finger. All these can communicate and be just as effective, sometimes more so, than a flood of words. Correction is also a part of communication and this is necessary for animals but also for students in school . . . and then let's never forget the praise when things are done right!

Finally *dominance* — yes, students must know that we are in control and that we must be obeyed. But we, in turn, are under the dominance of our Lord and Savior and I hope we are in a position that we can let our students know this and that they can see it in our lives.

So I wish Benny, Sandy, Shoshe, and Taffy well in their class which they have just begun. And I wish for all your Marys, Craigs, Sharons, and Davids a teacher who will be able to focus their minds on what he is saying, who will communicate effectively with them, and who will be able to secure the respect and obedience a teacher's position demands.

But I wish more than that for your students. I also wish for them a teacher who will be able to show them the importance of living a life fully submitted to the authority of God and of his Bible, and who will live the kind of Christian life that students will gladly emulate.

Dear Father, I thank you for the position of authority you have put me in. Help me to be worthy of this trust. Help me to be an effective teacher and one to whom students may look for guidance in the learning process. Most important, may they see Christ in me and, in turn, desire that I may see Christ in them. In your Son's name, Amen.

12
Supervision

Suggested Bible Reading: Proverbs 4:20–27

My son, pay attention to what I say;
* listen closely to my words.*
Do not let them out of your sight,
* keep them within your heart.*   [Prov. 4:20–21].

"You'd better come with me; I think I need some supervision," responded the four-year-old, as I suggested he take his rake and work in the back yard while I continued working in the front.

Little did he realize that my purpose in suggesting he continue by himself was to enable me to work faster, unencumbered by the well-meant but nevertheless work-slowing efforts of a preschooler. But I couldn't deny the little fellow's request and so the two of us continued raking leaves together, he under my supervision as he had requested and I gamely working around his efforts to be of help. "After all," I told myself, "just be thankful he desires supervision. The day will come soon enough that he will not be asking for adult help anymore."

During the next few days I could not forget Marty's request for supervision. I thought of the classroom where day after day teachers are called upon to supervise the work of their students, where they must continually tread the fine line between giving the students too much help so that they become overly dependent on an adult or making the mistake of not supplying help and guidance when it's really needed.

It is very true that one of the important qualities of a good teacher lies in being able to discern just how much help to give a student. For one, "help" may be in the form of, "I'm sure you can do that by yourself . . . go ahead and give it a try." For another it may be, "Here, let's do this together this time." But through it all we

29

must remember there comes a time when our opportunity to supervise and aid a student is past. This is true of the all-important attitudes and values which we seek to instill in our students, as much as in the teaching of facts and study skills.

Teachers, yours is a tremendous responsibility. I hope that daily you ask God to give you the sensitivity and the desire to mold your students' lives while you have the opportunity and while they are still receptive to your supervision. Remember to search daily for opportunities to guide them in the ways of the Lord.

> How shall the young direct their way,
>   What light shall be their perfect guide?
> Thy Word, O Lord, will safely lead,
>   If in its wisdom they confide.

God, sometimes my task overwhelms me, and it is then that I realize, all the more, my dependence upon you. May I be true to the trust placed in me and may I be able to give the proper supervision and guidance to those placed in my care. In Christ's name, Amen.

13
Choices

Suggested Bible Reading: Revelation 3:14–22

"I know your deeds, that you are neither cold nor hot. I wish you were either one or the other! So, because you are lukewarm —neither hot nor cold —I am about to spit you out of my mouth " [Rev. 3:15–16].

The proliferation of lawn signs in our city bears mute evidence to the fact that a political election is rapidly approaching. Having been involved as a volunteer campaign worker myself, I am aware of the last-minute planning that is going on, and the never-ending struggle to secure more finances which is taking place. I realize all the countless hours that volunteers, paid staff, and the candidate and his family are now putting in.

I guess that's why I pay particular attention to all the candidates' brochures that have arrived at my house and why I watch carefully the signs as they appear on lawns in my neighborhood. I find particularly intriguing three or four lawns within a few blocks of my house where two signs are placed side by side — each bearing the name of different candidates, vying for the same position. The fact that it is a nonpartisan election may make this easier to do — it would be more difficult to explain signs for a Democratic and a Republican candidate side by side on the same lawn!

But I do still wonder at the reason for these "two-candidate" lawns. Are the residents unwilling to hurt anyone's feelings by refusing to have a sign placed on their lawn? Are they uncertain themselves just which candidate they should support? Or is it perhaps a case of the husband supporting one candidate while the wife supports the other?

At any rate, the sight of these signs reminds me of Revelation 3:15–16. It is very true that there are times when it is difficult to make a choice, when the two sides both have merit and it seems as if a conscientious decision could go either way. Maybe that's the way the home owners feel about these candidates.

But there are many times when decisions can be made on clear-cut moral grounds or on the basis of right and wrong. As teachers and administrators we may have to make choices and take stands with which others do not agree, but knowing that we are letting God's precepts guide us should make this easier. After all, if God's Word is the norm for our lives it must also influence every decision we make, whether the consequences prove to be popular or unpopular with others. If God's rules are our guide, then our minds can be at ease, knowing that we have reached our conclusions and enforced our rules using God's Word as our standard. What better reason could we have for reaching the conclusions we do?

> Help us, Lord, when we are called upon to make decisions, to make them in the light of your Word. Let us clearly see what your will is. Then may we have peace of mind, regardless of the consequences, knowing that the action has been taken in a way which we believe is in accordance with your desire. For Jesus' sake, Amen.

14
"I Don't Get It!"

Suggested Bible Reading: Job 2:1 – 10

"You are talking like a foolish woman. Shall we accept good from God, and not trouble?" [Job 2:10].

I don't get it!"

"What don't you understand? What part is giving you trouble?"

"I don't know—I just don't get it!"

How often has an exchange of words similar to this taken place in your classroom? Have you experienced the same helpless feeling I have when, after you've explained something as carefully as you could, neither you nor the student is able to pinpoint the problem and the best he can do is shrug his shoulders, shake his head, and repeat, "I just don't get it!"

But students aren't the only ones whose response often is, "I don't get it." As adults there are many things we don't understand, that we "don't get." For example, some couples who would make excellent parents remain childless year after year; yet thousands of abortions are being performed every day. A talented minister in the prime of life dies; some patients in nursing homes long to be released from this life but linger on and on. A selfish, dishonest businessman prospers financially; his Christian counterpart has to close his business because he cannot pay his debts.

However, some things God is not going to reveal to us in this life. Think of Job and the many trials inflicted upon him. If ever anyone could say, "I don't get it" it would be he . . . and he probably never knew, in this life, why he was made to suffer as he did. Yet we, to whom the Bible has revealed the reason for Job's suffering, realize there was a good purpose behind this, for what could be more crucial than that God proves his point in a dispute with Satan?

It's a great comfort to know that our God makes no mistakes and that, even though there may be many events in this life that we do not understand, we still know he is in control and that he cares for us. "Are not five sparrows sold for two pennies? Yet not one of them is forgotten by God. Indeed the very hairs of your head are all numbered. Don't be afraid; you are worth more than many sparrows" (Luke 12:6–7).

May God grant us the faith to trust him and to accept whatever he gives us, knowing that it is for our good, even though we cannot understand why he allows these things to happen to us.

> Father in heaven, how grateful we are to know that you are caring for us and watching over us. How grateful we are that nothing happens to us without your permission. Help us, even when we do not understand, to place our trust and confidence in you, knowing that you are our loving Father and will allow nothing to happen to us that is not for our ultimate good. For Jesus' sake, Amen.

15
Love

Suggested Bible Reading: 1 Corinthians 13

"I have loved you with an everlasting love" [Jer. 31:3].

Do you love me?" eight-year-old Bobby repeatedly asked his foster parents, my sister and her husband. He lived with them for almost a year and throughout his stay the question was asked again and again. Often it was repeated at five- to ten-minute intervals, especially if it had just been necessary for his foster parents to reprimand or punish him.

They are happy that Bobby verbalized his insecurity and his need for constant reminders that he was loved and appreciated. If he had not done so, but had kept this need hidden, they would not have been able to reassure him whenever doubts arose in his mind (and many times in between!) that they cared for him and loved him.

I am sure you have had many Bobbys in your classroom who constantly demanded reassurances of your love and concern, even though it wasn't usually in the form of the direct question, "Do you love me?" For this need for attention and love can present itself in many ways: needing constant reassuring that work is being done correctly; misbehaving and deliberately trying to aggravate you as a teacher; just desiring to be near the teacher; perhaps recounting story after insignificant story, some true, others imagined. "Remember," our teacher's manual says, "it is the 'hard-to-love' child that needs the most love."

But there are other students who need our love and concern too. Today there are many children who are abused or who come from broken homes — certainly traumatic experiences for the boys and girls involved. It is true also that many children whose parents are in the process of securing a divorce blame themselves for the breakup of the marriage. What heavy burdens some of our students are bearing, and we teachers can feel so helpless in the face of these circumstances. Yet a willingness to listen, a ready smile, a word of encouragement, and an attitude of "I love you and I'm here to help you any way I can" will make the road easier for these students.

How fortunate is the child who has a sensitive teacher who recognizes this need for love. Not the wishy-washy, sentimental kind, but the kind that says, "I love you enough that I'm going to help you learn as much as you can while you are in my room. My love for you is going to be shown by a willingness to listen and by a genuine interest in you as a person, but also by my insistence — in a considerate and caring way — that rules be obeyed, that the rights of others be respected, and by seeing to it that you realize that punishment will follow disobedience."

Yet students aren't the only ones who need this caring and love. All of us as adults are just as needful of it and are just as vulnerable when it is lacking. Therefore, how comforting the words of God spoken through Jeremiah, "I have loved you with an everlasting love." Yes, even though we do not deserve it, even though our actions may seem to indicate that we do not want it, God's promise is there.

Bobby, because of his past experiences and uncertain future, felt compelled to ask, over and over, "Do you love me?" Not so for the Christian — we know God loves us; we have his Word and his Word is sure. May this promise strengthen and uphold us, just as our words of love and concern will strengthen and uphold our students.

> How thankful I am for your love, O Lord. May the many reminders and examples of your care toward me make my earthly journey pleasant and fruitful. Help me to be sensitive to my students' need for love and their need to be recognized as individuals worthy of their teacher's efforts and concern. May they always see Christ in me. In his name, Amen.

16
Our Country

Suggested Bible Reading: Deuteronomy 8:6– 20

When you have eaten and are satisfied, praise the LORD your God for the good land he has given you [Deut. 8:10].

There are many things, not specifically included in any course of study, which we still are able to teach our students. Sometimes this is done as an "extra" in the form of a special unit. Other times it involves an enlargement of some theme which we are already expected to teach. Or it may be that our personal attitudes and interests are apparent to our students and may have a real impact upon them.

But regardless of how it is accomplished, I hope that one of the values you will be able to pass on to your students is an appreciation for our country. It is not that our land is perfect and that there is no room for improvement. Far from it! There are black pages in our history, and even today there are injustices which must be righted and attitudes which must be changed. Nor must we hesitate to indicate these to our students. But, on the other hand, our nation has been abundantly blessed by God and we enjoy blessings and privileges denied to many. This must be impressed upon our students too.

Materially our nation is certainly abundantly blessed — we enjoy a standard of living which is unsurpassed by that of any other nation. But there are other blessings too. Our political system is stable and successful. Political campaigns are hard fought, but when the voting is finished there is no thought of rioting on the part of those who supported the losers or of jailing those who spoke out against the successful candidates.

The all-important freedom of religion which we enjoy, the liberty to speak out and write as we please, to organize and hold meetings when we desire — forbidden in many countries, but freely enjoyed by us — are all blessings of which our students should be aware. While many countries guard their borders night and day so that none of their citizens will escape, we must guard our borders so that citizens of other countries do not enter illegally!

One of our fourth graders, a Cambodian, helped our students realize in a vivid way what life can be like if these privileges are taken away. She wrote about some of her experiences. (Just previous to this the students had been studying about the troubles the Philistines brought upon the Israelites and she chose to term their oppressors "the Philistines.")

After explaining how the people were removed from the cities and sent to the country, she continued:

> When the Philistine leader became angry, he took the men, women, or babies to be killed. . . . Sometimes people talked to each other. The Philistine soldiers said, "You cannot talk to each other. If you do, I will kill all of you people." So the people were afraid when the Philistines said things like that.
>
> The people planted wheat and vegetables. . . . When the work was done the food was taken too. The people did not know where the Philistines were taking the food. . . .
>
> During the rule of Pol Pot, the children did not go to school, they just worked every day, the children worked from five years old to sixty years old. If they or the young people did not work they were killed. The people worked from 5 o'clock A.M. until 6 o'clock P.M.
>
> Some people tried to walk from Cambodia to Thailand and some succeeded. . . . Then the Thailand government called for help and then America came to take some people to America, Australia, and Canada. So more people were kept from being killed in Cambodia.

God grant it may never be necessary for us to experience what this fourth grader and her family did before we appreciate what God has given us in our land.

O Father of all nations, we are so grateful for what you have given us in our country. May we always thank you for it, and may we not become complacent. Help us to correct the wrongs which are still present and help us to continually reach out to those in other countries who are oppressed. May these people soon experience relief from the troubles which are theirs. In Christ, Amen.

17
Looking at the Heart

Suggested Bible Reading: Luke 16:10–16

. . . but God knows your hearts [Luke 16:15].

A group of eighth graders looks expectantly at me. Some appear very confident, others unsure of themselves. It is my task to distribute and monitor a Bible test while the regular teacher accompanies another class on a field trip.

After the handing out of papers and a few words of explanation, the room is quiet. All twenty-two students are working hard, the silence punctuated only by the scratching of pencils and the occasional shuffling of papers.

"How are they doing?" I wonder as I glance over the room. I'm sure their teacher could give a fairly accurate answer to this question, even before marking any of the papers. But for me, who knows the names of only a few of the students and much less their work habits and ability, looks can be very deceiving.

Ron, staring off into space, seems to be daydreaming. But perhaps he's plumbing the depths of his mind and his answers will reveal a maturity and understanding far beyond what one would expect of a thirteen or fourteen-year-old. Amy, brow wrinkled and a concentrated look on her face, is writing furiously. Yet she may be doing nothing more than addressing herself to everything but the questions, hoping that somehow the teacher will be impressed by the maze of words and will overlook that she really hasn't answered the questions at all.

No, I remind myself, things aren't always what they seem. I sometimes wonder about my colleagues too. The teacher who is always laughing and joking may actually be carrying a heavy burden on her heart. The one who can seem so quiet and withdrawn in the teachers' lounge may really blossom in the classroom and could well be exerting an outstanding, Christian impact on the lives of his students.

Let us, then, remember to look beyond outward appearances and make a real attempt to understand the inward motives and feelings of both our peers and our students. The results will be positive for all concerned!

Help me, Lord, not to judge others merely by outward appearances and actions. May I always remember that the words you spoke to Samuel when he was to anoint a king for Israel — "Man looks at the outward appearance, but [I] look at the heart" — are meant for me today just as much as they were for the prophet so many years ago. For your sake, Amen.

18
Work

Suggested Bible Reading: John 9:1–12

"Night is coming, when no one can work" [John 9:4b].

Isn't it wonderful to have work you enjoy so much that you can't wait for the holiday to be past so that you can get back at it?" my father asked on a Thanksgiving afternoon. Our family had just enjoyed a delicious meal, dishes were finished, and the adults were sitting around visiting and reminiscing. It might sound as if Dad did not enjoy our family visits, but this certainly was not the case. It was just that he, who had recently retired from teaching, was busily revising a book he had written earlier and was so immersed in it, was so thoroughly enjoying the work, that it was difficult to stay away from it.

I wonder how many of us have that much enthusiasm for our work. I must admit that I myself, although I love my work and wouldn't think of changing it for any other profession, am not always as eager for holidays to be past as my father was!

Yet if one doesn't thoroughly enjoy his work, I think it would be difficult to be a successful teacher. True, there are times when disappointments come and frustrations mount, but through it all we must not fail to realize that there are joys and rewards in the teaching profession that one seldom experiences in other careers. One of the tests of a successful teacher is the ability to remain enthusiastic about the work, absorbing the bumps and bruises that come along without becoming discouraged and disheartened.

"Burnout Figure High among U.S. Teachers, Sociologist Reports" read a headline in last week's newspaper. The article states that "nearly half of the teachers in U.S. urban schools feel 'burned out and trapped' in their jobs, according to a sociologist's study." The researcher also points out that older black teachers are the least likely to burn out. "They are more likely to feel they have a commitment to the community — to see their job as a calling," he reports.

This made me wonder: if a survey were conducted among only Christian teachers, would the "burnout rate" be any lower? If anyone would have a commitment to a cause, a vision to be fulfilled, it would seem to me it should be the Christian teacher. For what task could be more challenging than preparing students for the life ahead of them? What could be more stimulating than the training of those who someday will be the leaders in our world, our nation, our churches, and our homes?

So if the monotony of endless papers to mark, the discouragement of facing indifferent students, or the criticism of unreasonable parents gets you down, just remember what you are doing — preparing students for a lifetime of service, helping to mold and train tomorrow's leaders.

I hope that every one of you will experience as much joy in your work as my father did when he couldn't wait for the holiday to be over so that he could continue with the task God had laid out for him!

> Lord, thank you for work to do and the strength to do it. May I find joy in my work and see results from my efforts. May the words I speak and the way I act reveal to others that I am happy and thankful you have given me the privilege of working with your children. For Christ's sake, Amen.

19
Faithfulness

Suggested Bible Reading: Revelation 2:1 – 11

"Be faithful, even to the point of death, and I will give you the crown of life" [Rev. 2:10].

John is in exile on the isle of Patmos and he has been instructed by Christ to send messages to the seven churches of Asia Minor. The words quoted are part of the message Christ is sending to the church at Smyrna. He commends the Christians there for their faithfulness in the face of poverty and tribulation and then concludes his words to them with the challenge, "Be faithful, even to the point of death, and I will give you the crown of life."

Perhaps none of us will ever be tested "to the point of death," but I'm sure we all meet with temptations and tests which, if we fail them, would compromise our faithfulness to God, to his Word, and to the tasks he has given us. It's so easy to point out to others—including our students—what they should do and the way they should live, while at the same time, in the quiet of our own lives and homes, we often directly contradict what we have been instructing them to do. Yet this should not be!

In Edinburgh, Scotland, on a street named Candlemaker Row, there is a monument with a statue of a small Skye terrier atop it. The dog is gazing wistfully toward a cemetery in nearby Greyfriars Churchyard. He is affectionately known as Greyfriars Bobby and for fourteen years he had made this cemetery his home, for there was buried Auld Jock, his master. After following the small funeral procession to the churchyard, he resisted all efforts to provide a loving home for him, but chose instead to sleep on his master's grave, accepting food from the owner of a nearby restaurant as well as the undivided attention of the neighborhood children during the day.

But every night, year after year until his own death in 1872, found Bobby sleeping on Auld Jock's grave. Bobby was faithful not only until death, but even after the death of his master!

May we, in the position of responsibility God has given us, remain as faithful as this little dog in faraway Scotland. May we pray daily that our faithfulness may be genuine in our devotion to our fellow men and to the work God has given us to do, and especially that we may be true to God's Word and the standards he lays down for us in it. Then we too will some day experience the joys of which Christ spoke when he said, "I will give you the crown of life."

Dear Father, may we strive daily to live lives faithful to your infallible Word and to your commands. May we be able to interpret your Word correctly; then help us to faithfully pattern our lives after it. Forgive us when we give in to temptation and depart from the ways you command us to go. In Christ, Amen.

20
Rejected

Suggested Bible Reading: Romans 12:9–21

Be devoted to one another in brotherly love. Honor one another above yourselves. [Rom. 12:10].

Poison," she was called by many of her sixth-grade classmates. Whether she was ever called this to her face or not, I do not know . . . I hope not. But I do know she had to realize she was an outcast: never included in our friendly girl chatter, never asked to "stay over" at someone's house, always the last one picked when choosing sides.

True, the boys were more blatant in their mistreatment of her than we girls: refusing to touch anything she had touched or sit where she had sat without first blowing the supposed contamination from it, mocking those of us who—upon a rare occasion—made a feeble attempt to include her in some of our activities.

But then there came a time that she was absent from school. Reports were that she was in the hospital, a very sick girl. The prayers of our teachers and parents for her made a double impact upon us because we realized our attitude toward her had been so wrong. I know I—and I'm sure many of my classmates also—determined that if she recovered our actions toward her would have to change.

But such was not to be the case. After three days of hospitalization God took her home to heaven, leaving behind a mourning family and a group of guilty, conscience-stricken classmates.

The funeral I will never forget. There were ten girls left in our class and we were honorary pallbearers. The ten of us were to sing "We Are Going Down the Valley One by One," but after the first verse only one or two were able to continue. When the entire school sang "Safe in the Arms of Jesus" we fared somewhat better. At the cemetery we each placed a red rose on the coffin before it was lowered into the earth. But instead of spreading them out as we had been instructed to do, we bunched them all together on one end. That evening my mother excused me from practicing my piano lesson. "It's been a hard day for you, I know," she said. And she was right.

Since that time, and especially after I became a teacher myself, I have often wondered why our teachers didn't talk to us about our treatment of her. Perhaps they didn't realize the extent of our rejection, but they had to be aware, at least to a certain degree, of what was happening. And I like to think that if our unchristian actions (yes, this was in a Christian school) had been pointed out to us that at least some of us would have treated her better than we had been doing.

I'm not trying to excuse our actions by saying, "It was our teachers' fault; they should have made us change"; we knew better than to behave as we did. But I am suggesting that with the added pressure from a teacher I'm sure some of us would have tried to make life a little more pleasant for our classmate.

Teachers, be alert if any of your students are shunned or mistreated by their classmates. Speak to the students about this, show them how Christ would have treated such a person, and above all pray that such un-Christlike attitudes and actions do not exist in your classroom!

Forgive us, Lord, when we are thoughtless and inconsiderate of our fellow man. Help us to search out those who are lonely, who are mistreated, who are longing for a smile, a word of encouragement, or a gesture of friendship. May we be especially aware of any of our students who are the object of their classmates' ridicule or, at the very least, are ignored and shunned. May we, by example and word, show our students what the Bible means when it commands us, "Be devoted to one another in brotherly love." For Christ's sake, Amen.

21
Success

Suggested Bible Reading: Matthew 20:20–28

". . . the Son of Man did not come to be served, but to serve, and to give his life as a ransom for many" [Matt. 20:28].

If you have been in the teaching profession for a few years, it is interesting (and usually rewarding!) to inquire about your former students and see just where they are living now, what kind of families they have, and where they are working. Sometimes we hear reports that surprise us, but more often the patterns set in school and the traits displayed in the classroom are still evident when our former students take their place in the adult world.

When one inquires about former students, the reply may be, "Oh, Kim . . . she really has a good job," or "Dave is very successful." And then a list of the person's material goods and accomplishments is given. What disturbs me is that so often we Christians fall into the same method of categorizing success and "good jobs" as the non-Christian does. Almost without exception, a "good job" means one which pays well; being successful means heading a large company or earning the praise of men.

How often do we describe a person who has given himself or herself to do the Lord's work on some foreign mission field as having a good job, or the person who devotes his life to helping the "down and out" and aiding those who really need our help as being very successful?

I do not mean to belittle the person who is able to command a good salary or who holds an influential position in the eyes of the world. Those abilities, too, are gifts from God and if these people are Christians who are determined to let their light shine, they can accomplish much good for our Lord and his cause. But I am saying that we must not fall into the trap of judging a person's worth as the world does. Success and a good job mean much more than a large salary, a luxurious home, and fame in the minds of men.

In writing about the life of Christ, one of our junior-high students penned the following: "What impresses me most about the life of Christ and His ministry is that when Christ became human He didn't become wealthy or desire popularity. He came to serve." This student caught the meaning of true greatness, for this lies not in material possessions or in being popular and well-known, but in serving others, as Christ did. May we teachers seek to use this standard when evaluating the lives of others, including the lives of our former pupils. May we also be able to instill in the minds of our present students the truth that true greatness lies in serving others and not simply in amassing fame and fortune.

> Jesus Christ, thank you for the example you set for us, as well as for serving others. Help us to realize that this is where true greatness lies. May our lives show that we believe this and may we, by word and example, seek to point our students to this truth also. In your name, Amen.

22
Confession

Suggested Bible Reading: Psalm 32

When I kept silent,
my bones wasted away
through my groaning all day long [Ps. 32:3].

It's always been a temptation for me, if I'm short of money, to stick my bills in a drawer and forget about them. But that sure doesn't work; I found out the hard way," he admitted to me in one of his more candid moments. And I heartily agreed.

"Out of sight, out of mind" may be true sometimes, but one cannot will something out of existence by ignoring or forgetting about it. Whatever it is we're trying to avoid, to forget about, will not disappear just because we wish it would. You may bury that pack of time-consuming-to-mark papers in the bottom of your briefcase, but they will still be there tomorrow, and the next day . . . until you sit down and tackle the difficult task. That telephone call you know you must make to a critical, demanding parent will not be made until you pick up the phone and contact him. The misunderstanding you had with a fellow teacher will not be cleared up until one of you approaches the other and talks it out.

Neither will a guilty conscience be soothed by attempting to ignore it. King David found this out, but he also experienced blessed relief when he admitted his guilt and asked God for forgiveness.

Is there something that is bothering you today? It may be a small item—that file that needs cleaning or that bulletin board that needs changing. Or it may be a major item—a sin that needs confessing and forgiving, a reconciliation that needs to take place. Whatever it is, do not delay any longer. Remember that ignoring something will not make it disappear, and as long as it is there you cannot be as effective a teacher as you should be.

It's easy to shake our heads at the foolishness of a person stuffing his unpaid bills in the back of his dresser and trying to forget about them, but let's make sure that we aren't doing the same with things in our own lives.

Dear Lord, may I never be guilty of ignoring or attempting to forget things which should not be ignored or forgotten. Help me to seek forgiveness, to right any wrongs I can, and to live a life wholly dedicated to doing your will. For Jesus' sake, Amen.

23
Example

Suggested Bible Reading: John 13:1 – 17

"I have set you an example that you should do as I have done for you" [John 13:15].

It was a marvelous discovery which I as a third grader had made and I couldn't wait to get home to tell my mother about it. My teacher had long fingernails!

For weeks I had been begging my mother to allow me to let my fingernails grow. But no, our Saturday night bath ritual also included the trimming of fingernails and no amount of coaxing would persuade Mother to change her mind.

But now I had an irrefutable argument — Miss Vander Wall had long fingernails and if she did I certainly could have them too! So it was with new confidence that I burst into the kitchen with the announcement, "Guess what, Mom, Miss Vander Wall's fingernails are long. So now I may have them too, mayn't I?"

But Mother had an answer to this also. "When you're grown up and can keep your nails clean by yourself, you may have them as long as you want. But I'm sure that when your teacher was a third grader her nails were kept short also. So the answer is still no." End of discussion.

I'm sure Miss Vander Wall never realized what excitement the length of her fingernails caused in one of her students, and I often think of this in my association with students today. Who knows how much they are watching, imitating, and patterning their lives after us. I'm sure you've seen it in many ways: phrases you use in your classroom prayers are often used by the students in their prayers; the way you stand or walk, certain pet expressions, your facial expression . . . all are often mirrored in your students.

Doesn't this arouse within you a heightened sense of

responsibility, a new urgency demanding that you continually live the kind of life that is worthy of imitation?

Whether it's what you do with your leisure time, the TV programs you watch, the books you read, your reaction to some current event, your attitude toward your work and fellow teachers . . . all are being watched, consciously or unconsciously, by your students and are being imitated by them. Never forget that!

Thank you, Lord, for the privilege of training young lives. Help me to teach them all I can about the world you have placed us in, and help me to instill in them Christian attitudes and values. May I do this by carefully preparing my lesson plans, but help me to remember that students also learn from my actions and attitudes. May I strive daily to be a worthy example for them. In Jesus' name, Amen.

24
Decisions

Suggested Bible Reading: Proverbs 3:1– 20

Trust in the LORD with all your heart and lean not on your own understanding [Prov. 3:5].

It's a pleasant task but at the same time very difficult. It's interesting yet wearying, inspiring and at the same time frightening. It can be one of the most challenging parts of my work, yet I always breathe a sigh of relief when the task is completed.

I'm referring to the interviewing and subsequent appointment of prospective teachers. Many years ago the task was difficult because so few candidates were available. Today the task is equally difficult because there are so many excellent candidates.

And how do you know who to choose? There's the young person just graduating from college — enthusiastic, energetic, and eager to fulfill a lifelong dream of being a teacher. An "A" in student teaching . . . excellent recommendations from the college professors . . . topnotch scores from the hometown pastor . . . what more could you want?

But the next candidate is a mature woman — one with several years of teaching experience, who dropped out of her profession to rear her own family. Now that the youngest has just entered college she is eager to return to the classroom. Responsible, stable, an excellent, proven teacher . . . all qualities highly desired in any profession; she certainly would make an excellent addition to the staff also.

Then there's the graduate of our own school. He has been teaching elsewhere for a few years but now desires to be nearer friends and family. He's a person who knows the community and has earned its respect. The family has always been a staunch supporter of our school, even remembering it through prayers and financial gifts while they were living out of state. His qualifications, too, are excellent.

God's guidance has been asked by the chairman of the education committee before the interviews. Each candidate, you know, has prayed earnestly that he or she may be the one to receive the appointment. And now the decision is ours. It is an awesome task. One prays for the wisdom of Solomon . . . and for the candidates who will receive disappointing news.

Have you ever felt that a decision you must make may have a profound effect on someone's life? Should this student repeat a grade or will it be better if she is allowed to continue on with her classmates? Should you tell his parents about John's cheating on the test or do you hope that your discussion with him and his promise not to repeat his actions will suffice? What must you say when a parent asks you to discourage his son's or daughter's friendship with a problem student because he fears it may have a negative effect on his child, yet this student's friendship is just what the other person needs?

Well may we remember the words, "Trust in the Lord with all your heart and lean not on your own understanding." May this be the prayer of all of us . . . for the decisions we readily recognize as big and important, but also for the many small decisions which we must make day after day, both in the classroom and out of it. For often these "small" decisions accumulate and may even eventually be major, life-changing choices. God bless you in all your decisions!

Grant, Father in heaven, that I may continually look to you for guidance in all the decisions I must make. Help me to see your will clearly and then to be at peace with my decisions, knowing I have reached them carefully and conscientiously. For Christ's sake, Amen.

25
Graduation

Suggested Bible Reading: 1 Corinthians 13

And live a life of love, just as Christ loved us and gave himself up for us as a fragrant offering and sacrifice to God [Eph. 5:2].

Last week we had ninth-grade graduation. It's always fun to help the girls with their corsages, but it's even more fun to hear their remarks and comments to each other. "I just know I'm going to trip when I walk across the stage." "What a darling dress, Sheri ... I almost bought one just like it!" "Do you think my corsage is a little too high?" "Your mom made your dress, Karen? Boy, she's a good sewer." "One corsage left? What if two girls still have to come?" "I'm still mad at Mr. Wilkins for making me walk down the aisle with that pesky Bob!" And so the chatter goes on and on.

But are these the things that really are uppermost in their minds? I have a feeling that much of the talk is a cover-up for a tinge of sadness which is theirs, for the nervousness each one is experiencing, for the uncertainty of the future they face.

If we could get them to settle down for a moment and to reflect seriously on their past years of schooling I wonder what we would hear. I think it might be statements such as: "I'm acting big and brave, but I'm really scared silly of high school next year." "I'm awfully glad my parents said I had to be in by eleven tonight. I don't care to be out with the gang after that." "I really feel frightened when I think of the future. Am I going to be able to handle it?" "I sure hate to see my years of schooling here come to an end; I had a lot of good times."

I once asked a group of teen-agers to think back on the teachers they had had and to decide which one they remembered and appreciated the most, and why. The answers they gave were revealing. It was not, "He could really tell good stories . . . she hardly ever gave us homework . . . he let us get away with murder." No, the answers were, "You could tell he really cared about us . . . she was interested in each one of us as a person . . . she'd always take time to listen to us and to help us when we needed it . . . he really helped us learn a lot in his class." The teacher who was appreciated was the one who had a genuine interest in each student and who showed this in many ways throughout the day.

Isn't this just why our heavenly Father means so much to us? Because he cares for us and loves us he sent his only Son to die, thus gaining eternal life for us. It is the interest, the love, the concern that Christ shows to us and which we in turn as Christian teachers are required to show to our students that means so much to them and that they will remember long after graduation day.

Dear Christ, thank you for the love and concern you have for me. Thank you for dying on the cross for my sins, for preparing a place for me in heaven, and even for loving me enough to punish me when I do wrong. May my students see these same qualities in me as I work with them from day to day. In your name, Amen.

26
Wonderfully Made

Suggested Bible Reading: Psalm 139

I praise you because I am fearfully and wonderfully made;
  your works are wonderful,
  I know that full well [Ps. 139:14].

*W*onderfully Made is the title of a publication of Concordia Publishing House. It is a book about sex education written from the Christian viewpoint for boys and girls ages nine to eleven. The title is aptly chosen when one thinks not only of the reproductive system, but of all the other complicated body systems as well. The more science and the medical profession discover about the intricacies of the human body, the more man should stand amazed at the way our Creator has made us. When one considers how all parts of the human body are made to function together and how dependent the organs are upon each other, the wonder isn't that we become sick from time to time, but that we are well so much of the time!

And then to think that God has created all animals' bodies in just as marvelous a way. The plant world is also a marvel of God's creation and it too functions in a wonderful way. Yes, we have a marvelous God!

But yet we have with us some whose bodies and minds, as a result of sin in the world, do not function as they should. There are with us both children and adults whose minds may be keen and alert, but whose bodies are crippled and handicapped . . . or those whose bodies are healthy but whose minds are incapable of functioning in a normal manner. How we should thank God for our normal minds and bodies, also asking him that we may treat these "special" people with understanding and respect, with love and concern.

The year 1983 was designated the "Year of the Disabled Child." It is well that the needs of these children and

58

their families are called to our attention, for too often they are overlooked or avoided. Some of you may have had such a child in your room, perhaps the result of the recent trend of "mainstreaming." If you did, or if you do in the future, I hope you will view it as an opportunity to help one who is not as fortunate as the other students in your room and as one whom God has placed under your care for a special purpose. What a beautiful way to teach other students to be tolerant of all children, including those with handicaps, and to appreciate their own healthy minds and bodies.

Yes, we are fearfully and wonderfully made . . . let us never forget to acknowledge our Maker and to thank him for the wonders of our bodies!

Dear Lord, thank you for making us in such a wonderful way. Thank you, also, for medical science which helps us understand the way you have created us and which is able to help us when our bodies do not function as they should. May we always be understanding of those who are sick or disabled, helping them and supporting their families as much as we can. For Jesus' sake, Amen.

27
Change

Suggested Bible Reading: Isaiah 40:1 – 11

The grass withers and the flowers fall,
but the word of our God stands forever [Isa. 40:8].

There are some things in our day-to-day school life that do not change much. The loss of a tooth is still a major event for a first grader. Giggly fourth graders bound for a birthday party are still as excited as their counterparts would have been fifty years ago; the first snowfall brings an excitement and restlessness to even the "sophisticated" senior-high students; and a new pair of shoes still brings joy to at least some students. ("Who cares about that?" asked a kindergarten student as the teacher was trying to elicit a discussion with the five-year-olds. "I got a new pair of shoes yesterday!")

Yet if there is one thing people the world over would agree on it is that we live in a world of change — change so rapid that science textbooks are almost out of date before they are off the press. Futurists are making predictions which seem impossible, yet some of these predictions are already starting to come true.

My mother often speaks of the changes she has seen in her lifetime: of the time they were sewing her sister's wedding dress and they carelessly threw it on the floor to rush outdoors to catch a glimpse of an automobile passing by, of the thrill she gave her students a few months later as she took many of them for their first automobile ride in her father's new car, or of the sixty students she taught one year in grades one through four. Yes, our senior citizens have witnessed enormous changes in their lifetime, and the rate of change has accelerated so tremendously that who knows what changes we, and much more our students, will see in the years ahead.

What a comfort the words of Isaiah — "the word of our

God stands forever" — can be to us Christians. The fast pace of change in today's world, especially when we wonder how we can prepare our students for life in such a world, can leave us bewildered and fearful. But then to know that our God never changes, that his love for us is ever the same, that his Word to us — the holy Bible — is still his inspired, infallible message can give us strength for today and hope for tomorrow.

What a blessed future is ours!

Thank you, dear Father, for your Word that never changes and for your promise that you will never change either.

Change and decay in all around I see,
O Thou who changest not, abide with me.
In your Son's name, Amen.

28
Kindness

Suggested Bible Reading: Ephesians 4:17 – 32

Be kind and compassionate to one another   [Eph. 4:32].

We were rather surprised when Carl did not show up for school on that first day. Perhaps the rumor was true, after all, that he had left our school for another one. But it was difficult to understand why. Academically he did very well; he always seemed to have an abundance of friends; the teachers also spoke well of him. Tuition should have proved to be no problem for his parents.

So, out of curiosity, I checked his records and in one sentence, written by last year's teacher on the parent-teacher conference sheet, found what could be the reason: "Carl's parents say he is very conscious of his size and some students have teased him about this in the past; I said I would do my best to put a stop to this."

Perhaps I was jumping to an unwarranted conclusion when I felt I may have found the reason for Carl's transfer, but permit me to let my mind wander and to reconstruct what might have happened.

Carl, tall for his age and somewhat overweight, was well liked by his classmates. I'm sure no one would have hurt him intentionally. So what was said was said in jest and nothing malicious was meant by it. But yet it cut and hurt, so much that he did not wish to return to our school and had persuaded his parents to allow him to attend another school, hoping that new acquaintances and different friends would be kinder and would not, even in a joking way, make fun of his size. True? I don't know . . . but I'm convinced this could well have happened.

"Be kind and compassionate to one another." Yet so often our students—yes, even Christian boys and girls—ignore this command of God and make life miserable for

62

one another. It hurts me particularly when I see them poking fun of physical disabilities of others: imitating the walk of a child who has cerebral palsy, mocking the speech impediment a classmate may have, poking fun of the near-sighted or cross-eyed child, making snide remarks about the color of someone's skin — or the tallness or shortness of a classmate.

What an opportunity for us to impress our students with the importance of understanding and tolerance for others, while at the same time teaching them to be thankful for the "normalcy" which is theirs. In a direct way a teacher must try to overcome these attitudes, words, and actions. But in an indirect way much can also be done: reading stories about handicapped people — especially those told from the handicapped person's view — and then discussing the story together. We can show concern and talk about our own concern for those with problems; we should stress to students that everyone is different and that all have a worth and dignity which must be respected . . . that being different or having a handicap does not mean being inferior.

Once again a teacher can play a major role in shaping children's attitudes. May you never be too busy or too immersed in making lesson plans and marking papers that you fail to continually remind students of God's command, "Be kind . . . to one another."

Dear God, help me to be kind and compassionate to others and help me to teach my students to show this kindness also. Forgive me when I fail to watch for students who may be ignoring this command, or when I fail to show kindness in my own life. In Christ's name, Amen.

29
Answered Prayers

Suggested Bible Reading: Psalm 139

Search me, O God, and know my heart;
test me and know my anxious thoughts [Ps. 139:23].

If it were in your power to fulfill an eleven-year-old's prayer request you would, wouldn't you?" The words, spoken by my brother, had an ominous ring to them and I answered guardedly, "Probably . . . but I don't quite trust this. What's it all about?"

"Well, last night Kris concluded her prayer by saying, 'And, God, please make Aunt Hester brave enough to go on the cable car tomorrow.' "

I was on a three-week camping trip in Europe with my brother, his wife, and their two children. For them the trip up the mountain near Andermatt was to be a highlight of our experience in Switzerland. Yet I had gladly volunteered to guard our rented van and its contents while the rest of the family enjoyed a ride on the swinging, swaying cable car!

For one whose palms sweat before every airplane take-off and who would rather pay five dollars to stay off the roller coaster than to go on it, my offer to guard the van and its contents could hardly be called a sacrifice. Yet to cause the prayer of an eleven-year-old to be answered negatively was not to be done lightly either. So, an hour after breakfast all five of us were entering the cable car for our thirty-minute trip up the mountain. True, I found a seat as far from the windows as possible, and I studied the floor very intently all the way up and most of the way down. Yet the view from the top — windy, cold, and frost-covered — was one I will never forget. It was well worth the experience.

I am thankful Steve clued me in on the prayer of his daughter that night in Switzerland — thankful because it was in my power to have her prayer answered in a positive way. Since then I have found myself thinking, "How good it would be if we could know all the requests which our students send heavenward and which involve us as their teachers."

"Lord, help my teacher to understand I feel bad because I'm not as smart as my brother." "Please, God, I want to make the basketball team. Help the coach to choose me." "God, why did Ann make the cheerleading squad and not me? She's in so many things already." "Lord, I've studied so hard for my history test; help me to get a passing mark."

But on second thought, I'm glad God doesn't let us know what all these requests are because we can't always answer them positively. Not everyone can make the basketball team or the cheerleading squad; even the most competent teacher cannot assure every student a passing grade.

Instead the solution is that we be constantly tuned in to the feelings and emotions of our students. Just as the psalmist in Psalm 139 asked God to know his thoughts, so may we ask God to help us constantly be aware of the thoughts and feelings of our students. If we but think of it, we know those cut from choir or the volleyball team are going to be disappointed. We know it isn't a good feeling to have a brother or sister who is a better student or more popular than you are. Every sensitive teacher will realize these students need special understanding, even if it's no more than a listening ear and a genuine interest in them. May you be that kind of teacher!

Help me, Lord, to be attuned to students' feelings and to gladly offer sympathetic understanding whenever it is needed. May the things I do and say, outside the classroom as well as in it, help the students to realize I have a sincere, personal interest in them, and that I understand their disappointments as well as their joys. For Jesus' sake, Amen.

30
Obedience

Suggested Bible Reading: Matthew 23:23 – 28

On reaching Jerusalem, Jesus entered the temple area and began driving out those who were buying and selling there. He overturned the tables of the money changers and the benches of those selling doves, and would not allow anyone to carry merchandise through the temple courts   [Mark 11:15 – 16].

The moment I walked into the supervised study hall, I knew it wouldn't work . . . Gregg and Tom at the same table. It had been tried before, but their friendship was too strong and their willpower too weak to allow them to accomplish anything productive while sitting that near each other.

So I walked over to them and said, "Will one of you move to another table? I'm sure you'll accomplish much more if you're not so close to each other." They smiled, knowing full well how right I was, and I returned to my desk.

However, two minutes later they were still in the same spot and seemingly had no intention of following through on my request. So I went back to them. "I asked one of you to move. Why haven't you done so?"

"Well," was the response, "we didn't know who should move. You didn't tell us."

So I replied, "All right, Gregg, you come and sit by this table." He immediately did so and the study hall proceeded smoothly, with both boys apparently making real progress in completing their assignments.

As I returned to my desk the thought struck me that eighth graders still need careful guidance and direction. For some at least, even the decision of who should move to a different spot is one they apparently cannot or at least do not wish to make. So then an adult has to make it for them.

It is good for adults to live within certain limits and to have rules which must be obeyed. Then certainly this is true for our students. Let's not be afraid to let them know what our rules are and that punishment will follow if these are ignored or disobeyed.

Our supreme example, Christ himself, was full of love and compassion, yet he certainly was not afraid to speak out. Think of how he addressed the Pharisees in Matthew 23 and how he fearlessly drove the moneychangers out of the temple.

So let us as teachers be conscious of students' feelings — of their fears or their hopes — but at the same time let us not hesitate to correct whenever necessary and to punish when rules are disobeyed or ignored.

I am grateful, Lord, that you have placed me in a position of authority. Help me to use this in the right way. May I not be afraid to set limits and to insist that rules be followed. But give me wisdom to make just rules and then help me to enforce them in a kind, understanding way. In Jesus' name, Amen.

31
Death

Suggested Bible Reading: Psalm 116

For this God is our God for ever and ever;
he will be our guide even to the end [Ps. 48:14].

Mommy, does it hurt much to die?" asked a third grader one day. And this was no idle question. Cathy was suffering from a serious heart condition, the result of an illness a few years earlier. That she realized the seriousness of her condition was shown by the question she asked her mother, a question which undoubtedly arises in the mind of many.

"It's not that I'm afraid of death." It was a senior citizen speaking. "I know I'm going to heaven and I know it will be wonderful there. But it's what may happen to me before death comes that sometimes bothers me. Will I become a burden to my children . . . will I suffer a lot of pain . . . will I linger on and on in a nursing home?" Young children, old people—all have questions about death and dying.

Yet the moment of our death, and the manner of it, is one of the things God has chosen not to reveal to us. Nor has he given us many details about heaven beyond the fact that it is a most beautiful place, with not a trace of suffering or sadness. "No eye has seen, no ear has heard, no mind has conceived what God has prepared for those who love him" (1 Cor. 2:9).

The rest we must accept by faith, and for the Christian that should be enough. Yes, it is human nature to desire to know what God has in store for us and our loved ones, yet we must be content to put that in the hands of God, knowing that he is our all-wise, all-loving Father. After all, if he has all the hairs of our heads numbered (Matt. 10:30; Luke 12:7), we can also trust him to provide for us, both in this life and the life to come.

And Cathy, the third grader of whom I spoke? It was not God's will that she enter heaven as a young child. She is now a vivacious teen-ager, living carefully it is true, but nonetheless happy and active . . . God's time for her is not yet and for this we praise him!

Father in heaven, help me to accept whatever you have in store for me and my loved ones. May I live in faith and not in fear, knowing that when my life on earth is done you will take me home to heaven, there to live with you forever. In Christ, Amen.

32
Don't Give Up!

Suggested Bible Reading: Ecclesiastes 11:1–6

Cast your bread upon the waters,
for after many days you will find it again [Eccles.
11:1].

He was a year or two behind me in school, but since
it was a small school which had two or three grades to
a teacher we often were in the same room. Looking back
on it now, I realize how many headaches he must have
given his teachers, and we as his classmates were no help
either, for I fear we often encouraged him in his mis-
behavior. Learning seemed to be difficult for him; par-
tially to make up for this lack, he became the class clown
and the class cutup—and all of us loved it. I imagine our
teachers were ready to give up on him several times and
often wondered what ever would become of Bob.

Even though we eventually moved out of state, I still
was able to keep in touch with several of my former
classmates and so when I heard that Bob was living in
Colorado, I decided to contact him when I was in the
area. And I'm glad I did. In fact, I wish our teachers—
especially our history and geography teachers—could
have shared my experience.

The first thing Bob and his wife did when they heard
I was near them was to change their plans for the day
and arrange to take us, in their four-wheel-drive vehicle,
back into the mountains in areas where no vehicles or-
dinarily traveled. This turned out to be one of the best
and most interesting "guided" tours I have ever taken.
Our social-studies teachers would have been surprised
and delighted to hear all the history and geography Bob
related to us. Here was a person who in school couldn't
have cared less who settled where or what caused a particular turn of events, now giving us one fascinating fact

after another about the area we were driving through
. . . and that with an animation and interest that could
not be improved upon. I found myself thinking, "Is this
the same Bob I knew back in school in Iowa?"

Was it a particular teacher who whetted his appetite
for all the information he so effectively gave us, or was
it just a gradual maturing process that took place? At any
rate, this experience taught me that we must never give
up on any students, that we must continue to work with
them, to pray for them, and to show a real interest in
them. For even the most rebellious, the most mischie-
vious, the one who seems the most resistant to learning
of any kind may have a real change of heart and later in
life will come to appreciate all the efforts you put forth
for him or her.

> Dear Lord, help me to look beyond the petty irritations
> and discouragements of today. May I realize that I never
> know what impression my words will make upon my
> students and how my actions and attitudes of today may
> affect the lives of my students in all the tomorrows which
> will be theirs. Forgive me when I become impatient and
> help me to show your love toward even the most unlov-
> able. For Jesus' sake, Amen.

33
Happiness

Suggested Bible Reading: Psalm 100

Rejoice in the Lord always. I will say it again:
Rejoice! [Phil. 4:4].

Recently I attended a seminar on leadership where the speaker said it has been proven that effective leaders are happy and laugh often . . . that laughter can help facilitate the achievement of goals. Some people even call the ability to laugh about one's circumstances a "survival skill." At least eighteen books, he said, have been written during the last few years in which the case is made that laughter is a physical healer and that there is even some evidence showing a correlation between laughter and the prevention of illness.

Small wonder, then, that our Lord, who created us and made us as we are, speaks so often about joy and happiness in the Bible: "I will be glad and rejoice in you . . . O Most High" (Ps. 9:2); "A happy heart makes the face cheerful" (Prov. 15:13); "Therefore my heart is glad and my tongue rejoices" (Acts 2:26); "The upright see and rejoice" (Ps. 107:42); "Serve the Lord with gladness" (Ps. 100:2); "But we had to celebrate and be glad" (Luke 15:32).

The Bible leaves no doubt in our minds that God wants us to be happy and to show it. One of the encouraging things about it is that a smile and a happy outlook can spread so easily to others. The happiness of a friend, shared with you and others, soon multiplies. A friendly manner and ready smile from the cashier at the grocery store or the nurse attending your sick husband or wife can do much to buoy one's spirits. In school also, a happy outlook and an encouraging smile can be worth many words. A smile, as she leaves for home, for the student you had to punish speaks volumes to her. A reassuring smile to apprehensive parents who have been called in for a conference has a positive effect; a cheerful demeanor in the teachers' lounge can do much for the morale of the entire staff.

A teacher who radiates happiness and joy in the classroom will find the same attitude reflected. "I like my teacher. She's glad to me," is the way one youngster phrased it.

How thankful we should be that as Christians we do not have to fake happiness and laughter. For, even though we have our disappointments and hardships and may at times be overwhelmed by sadness, underneath it all we have something that others cannot have. "Rejoice *in the Lord,*" Paul tells us. And we can do just that, for ours is the happiness of a living hope, of a secure comfort, and of a triumphant faith. What more could we want and what more do we need as we work and live — in joy and happiness — for Christ here below?

> Thank you, heavenly Father, for desiring happy Christians and for giving me so many reasons for happiness. May my joy be shown in all I do and say, and may this joy be abundant evidence to others of the happiness that comes when a person's life is fully committed to you. In your Son's name, Amen.

34
God's World

Suggested Bible Reading: 1 Timothy 6:3 – 21

> . . . *who richly provides us with everything for our enjoyment* [1 Tim. 6:17].

Our third graders have been busy studying the five senses. It is a beautiful way to introduce them to God's world and to show them how they may enjoy it. How much those are missing who do not thrill to the sight of a beautiful sunset or the brilliant red of a maple tree in the fall of the year, who hardly notice the smell of a newmown lawn or the fragrance of a rose. What pleasure they are denying themselves who do not hear music in the babble of a brook or sense God's power as they hear the rolling thunder, or for whom the taste of a peach plucked straight from the tree or a tomato gleaned fresh from a backyard garden is unknown. Those who do not know the touch of a soft, furry puppy or the feel of rain splashing on their faces are certainly missing some of life's real joys.

A wonderful opportunity is ours as teachers to help heighten our students' awareness of the blessings God gives us through the world of nature and of the senses he gives us so that we may enjoy his world. What an opportunity to remind students — and ourselves as well — that so many of the joys in life need not be expensive, that, in fact, many of them are free. All we need is to be conscious of the world around us, to look and listen for the beauty which is there, and then to sharpen our senses so that we may make the most of what our Maker has provided for us.

Neither should we pass by the opportunity to teach children the importance of good stewardship. How important it is that we instill in them a desire to take care of God's world, not using it for our own benefit, but to

74

realize we are merely caretakers of God's world and that he expects us to use the resources he has given us carefully and wisely.

It is not difficult to motivate young children to discover and enjoy the world around us. In the fall, ask them to bring pretty leaves to school and you will soon have a forest. In the spring, a call for polliwogs or tadpoles will result in an aquarium full of them. A call for "anything interesting" in the world of nature will result in a myriad of items from dead birds to stones to cast-off snakeskins. How wonderful is the enthusiasm of a child! May we adults show this same enthusiasm and appreciation, and may we be able to encourage this interest and excitement on the part of our students so that when they reach adulthood they may continue to thank our God "who richly provides us with everything for our enjoyment."

Creator of heaven and earth, we thank you for the world you have given us. For, even though as a result of man's sin it is no longer a perfect world, there is still much beauty in it. We thank you for the senses which are ours so that we may enjoy your world. Help us always to be good stewards of it; may we realize it is not ours to exploit for our own benefit, but that we are merely caretakers for you. In our Father's name, Amen.

35
Homes

Suggested Bible Reading: Romans 12

We have differing gifts, according to the grace given us [Rom. 12:6].

The three o'clock bell has rung and immediately the quiet, deserted halls are turned into a sea of children's faces. It's a study in human nature to watch the students go past: Lisa, the worrier, intent on only one thing—getting outdoors on time so she won't miss her bus; friendly Gary, face wreathed in smiles as he walks past with a cheerful, "Good-by, see you tomorrow!"; energetic Bob, tempted to run . . . skipping around his classmates, slowing down only when he sees I have my eyes on him. Then finally there comes Dave, plodding along, never in a hurry. As he strolls past I wonder if this was another one of those days when he almost drove his teacher to distraction by not completing any of his work on time.

But my mind travels to other things and I wonder just what type of home each of the students will be returning to. Some will go to spacious houses, professionally decorated and elegantly furnished, while others live in small, crowded quarters furnished with the castoffs of others. Some go home to a lonely life—an only child perhaps with both mother and father working. Others find a houseful of people—so busy and noisy that even finding a place to do homework creates a problem. Some will return to homes where mother and father are constantly arguing; others retreat to a place where love abounds and where real concern for each other is evidenced.

For some the conversations at mealtime center only on financial matters and how more money may be made; in others it is a recital of complaints about Dad's boss, John's teacher, and Mother's former friend who won't speak to her anymore. Yet others will benefit from a really stimulating conversation, one which helps to broaden their interests, to increase their knowledge, and to heighten their concern for those who are not as blessed as their family is.

What a challenge is ours as, from day to day, we face these students from such diverse backgrounds and with such differing gifts and personalities. May all of them find, in our classrooms, a place of joy and contentment, of challenge and reward, of orderliness and consistency, so that — regardless of the type of home that is theirs — they will remember our classroom as one that equipped them well for the years God will give them on this earth.

Thank you, Lord, for allowing me to mold these young lives from day to day. Help me to be conscious of the many different personalities and gifts and the backgrounds they represent, as well as the many different homes to which they return each day. May I be able to reach each one of them in a way that prepares them well for their life ahead. For Jesus' sake, Amen.

36
Computers

Suggested Bible Reading: Proverbs 3:1 – 18, 27

All this I tested by wisdom and I said,
  "I am determined to be wise" —
    but this was beyond me [Eccles. 7:23].

This is an experience every teacher should have," I said to myself as I struggled through a computer course recently. It didn't take me long to realize, as I sat in the class, that I was out of my element. It seemed as if everyone had had some previous experience with the machines or at least had a husband who knew all about them! And I sat there hardly knowing the difference between a TRS-80 and an Apple, let alone how to get them to follow all the instructions as they're supposed to do. Talk of input and output, bits and bytes, chips and bugs left me bewildered and confused.

Anyone who has worked for hours trying to get the computer to follow some "simple" command, only to find she was inserting a period when it should have been left a space, or putting in only one space when it should have been two, will understand some of the frustration I experienced.

Sometimes when I was in class I would wonder, "Is this the way some of my students have felt in the past?" As I sat there, trying hard not to look too mystified, I would think, "Tomorrow I'll check this out with Craig or Dave" — our school's "computer experts" who so patiently guided me through the course, even enabling me to pass it eventually with flying colors!

But why wish an experience like this on my fellow teachers? It's because I'm sure it will make them better teachers. Most of those in the teaching profession were undoubtedly average or better-than-average students themselves and struggling through a class, or having a difficult time understanding what the teacher was trying to explain, is probably a foreign experience to them. We may do our best to empathize with the slow students and perhaps may even succeed at doing so, but we will be all the better equipped to do so if we can recall some experience we had personally. Perhaps it will make us more patient when students fail to understand the point of the lesson; it should make us more willing — or even eager — to spend time outside of class giving extra explanations to those who are experiencing difficulty.

My father, after many years in the parish ministry, accepted a position as a seminary professor. Although he still occupied the pulpit fairly regularly as a guest minister, he also found himself sitting in the pew more often than previously. His remark was, "People would be much better preachers if they were able to sit through church services more often themselves."

There is much truth in the saying, "Never criticize a person until you have walked a mile in his moccasins." But if this is not possible, let us pray daily that God will give us the ability to understand our students' frustrations and fears. Then may we, in love and concern, willingly seek to help them in any way we can. "Do not withhold good from those who deserve it, when it is in your power to act" (Prov. 3:27).

> Dear God, help me to be aware of the problems my students may have — whether they be academic, social, or spiritual. May I be able to put myself in their place and thus be able to help them better as they sit in my classroom and walk the school's halls from day to day. In Christ, Amen.

37
Judging

Suggested Bible Reading: Matthew 7:1 – 12

"Do not judge, or you too will be judged"   [Matt. 7:1].

It was during the fall of 1917 and World War I was still raging. My mother was teaching grades four, five, and six in a Christian school in a small town in Iowa. Most of the supporters of the Christian school were of Dutch descent and, since Holland was not involved in World War I, this caused the non-Dutch people of the community to spread rumors that these "Dutch people" were German sympathizers. The proximity of Holland to Germany and the similarity of the two languages did nothing to allay the suspicions of the community either.

As a result, instances of harassment against the Christian-school community were common. Mother recalls well the day when she arrived at school to find a large, black sign across the door with the white letters *CLOSED* boldly painted on it. She also remembers the time when the students from the public school marched over to her school and grouped around the flagpole. Teachers and students in the Christian school were asked to come outdoors and join in singing the national anthem. Realizing the touchy situation and what could be the consequences if they refused, the entire student body with their teachers complied. At the conclusion of the anthem students from both schools returned to their respective classrooms.

But the climax was reached one morning when the minister, who had arisen early to finish preparations for the funeral of a young soldier who had fallen victim to the flu epidemic, suddenly noticed flames in the basement of the Christian school. The "Americans" had succeeded in breaking into the school and starting a fire by igniting crumpled-up papers they had placed under

Mother's desk. The result was that the fire had burned through the floor; the desk dropped into the basement where it had continued burning until spied by the minister. Quick action resulted in the fire being extinguished before too much damage was done. The next day, however, a sympathetic mayor declared all schools, both public and Christian, closed due to the flu epidemic and declared them open again only when the fire damage had been fully repaired.

Yes, what a disruption there can be and what antagonisms can be aroused just because someone, or some group, unfairly judges others and lays blame on those who deserve no blame at all. For the people being harassed were just as patriotic, just as loyal to their country as those who so self-righteously were doing the harassing.

Do we ever find any of this in our own lives and in our own classrooms? You may have heard a remark about a certain student or about his or her parents, about another teacher, about your principal or some board member . . . and if we aren't careful we accept it as the full truth and allow it to control our thoughts and to affect our actions as they relate to the parties involved. We never think of checking for ourselves to see if the information is correct. How unfair and unfortunate this is.

May God give us the desire to search out for ourselves just what the facts are and the sensitivity to realize what damage may be done by blindly accepting whatever rumor we may hear. May we have the wisdom to know how to deal with these unfair, often untrue and exaggerated accusations and insinuations.

We ask, Lord, that we may never hastily jump to conclusions or that we may never allow words spoken without substantiation to control our thoughts and our actions. May we always carefully weigh the facts and make deliberate, conscientious decisions. Help us to remember the command of Jesus that we "do not judge, or [we] too will be judged." Forgive us when we fail. For Christ's sake, Amen.

38
Good-bys

Suggested Bible Reading: Acts 20:17 – 38

They all wept as they embraced him and kissed him. What grieved them most was his statement that they would never see his face again. Then they accompanied him to the ship [Acts 20:37 – 38].

Five o'clock on the last day of school. As I walk down the deserted halls I have an empty feeling in the pit of my stomach. Just this morning the halls were filled with hundreds of youngsters — eager and happy, looking forward to their summer vacation. And now the halls have changed dramatically: in some places the custodian has already emptied the classrooms so that floors may be cleaned and waxed. The result is that one has to thread his way through student and teacher desks, filing cabinets, and bookcases.

In other places the monotony of the halls — now devoid of student artwork and attractive bulletin-board displays — is broken only by a crippled globe, an out-of-date wall map, and a box of books which the teacher has deemed beyond repair. "Discard" say the notes the teachers have placed on these items.

I often wish I weren't so sentimental and that saying good-by weren't so difficult for me. I guess that's why I'm relieved when the last day of school is over, for the good-bys can be many: to fellow workers who will not be returning when school opens, to students who are graduating or who will be transferring to other schools. The classroom teacher feels this even more intensely, for even though this year's students may be right across the hall next year, they will "belong" to someone else and the relationship will never be the same again. Yes, the last day of school is a day of good-bys.

One of the joys of heaven will be that we will never

have to say good-by to anyone, will never have to think, "Will I ever meet this person again?" or "What will happen to us before we see each other again?" I imagine that Paul and all those who wept because he had told them they "would never see his face again" looked forward to heaven for the same reason.

The empty feeling is still with me as I arrive home that night, but I know it will change. Monday morning I'll be back in school. The halls will still be deserted, more desks will clutter the halls, even the bells which so control the lives of students and teachers will be silent. But the empty feeling will be gone. After we tie up a few loose ends from the past year, our attention is turned to the coming year. There are books to be ordered, class lists to be reviewed, plans to be laid . . . all looking ahead to another year of service for God and for his precious children.

Isn't that one of the joys of life? Yes, there are disappointments and regrets, there is pain and suffering, but there is always another day. Today's pain will be more tolerable tomorrow, today's mistakes will help us avoid other errors in the future, and today's disappointment will turn out to be God's appointment. How thankful we should be that we can look beyond today, even when we are discouraged, trusting God for whatever he has in store for us.

We are grateful, Lord, for the ability to look beyond today's good-bys and disappointments and to look forward with anticipation to whatever you have in store for us. We are especially thankful for the perfect life we will someday experience in heaven. Help us to pass this vision on to our students. In Christ, Amen.

39
Tomorrow

Suggested Bible Reading: Psalm 90

Teach us to number our days . . . [Ps. 90:12].

So long, see you tomorrow!" How often we repeat these words to our students as they leave for the day or to our fellow teachers as we meet them in the hall, ready for the trip home and a few moments of relaxation before getting back to the marking of papers and the preparation of lesson plans for the next day.

But God's ways are not always our ways. A casual "so long" to Marian, a friend and colleague for seventeen years, on that Monday afternoon became a "So long, see you in heaven" — not the "see you tomorrow" we had so often said to each other. For before she reached home, due to slippery road conditions, her car was hit broadside by a pick-up truck and within two hours she was at home with her Lord.

It was a somber, subdued group of teachers that met briefly the next morning in the elementary-school library before school started. After a short prayer and a few words from Scripture we left for our classrooms and offices, each breathing a prayer of our own for the twenty-eight fourth graders whose teacher had been taken from them so suddenly, for the substitute teacher who had a very difficult spot to fill, and for the aged mother who could no longer look forward to her daughter's return every afternoon.

We could not help but be aware that this was the third time within four short months that God had spoken to our school community through accidental death. First it was the father of three of our students who was killed instantly when a drunk driver crossed the center line and hit, head-on, the van in which he was riding; next a vision technician who had served our school for several years was killed while driving from one school to another; and now a deeply loved, highly respected fourth-grade teacher was suddenly called home.

When sorting through her belongings (how much can accumulate through a seventeen-year span of teaching!) I came across a piece of tagboard on which she had lettered the words, "All to the Glory of God." Often I had seen this displayed prominently in her room, for this was truly her motto and one which she desired earnestly to have her students claim as their own. If she could have one message for us who still have so many opportunities for influencing the lives of young people day after day I am sure it would be, "No one knows how much more time God will give you to use your influence in molding young lives. So use every moment you have, seize every opportunity that presents itself to guide your students in the ways of the Lord, helping them to see the all-importance of doing 'all for the glory of God.' "

Dear Lord, thank you for the opportunity you give us, day after day, to help mold young lives. Help us to make the most of each moment because we never know which day and which hour may be our last. In our Father's name, Amen.

40
Some Reflections on Psalm 23

The LORD is my shepherd,
I shall lack nothing.

Just think — the Creator of everything, Master of the universe, the King of kings, is my Shepherd. He cares for me, knows me by name, binds up my hurts, and searches for me if I am lost! No wonder King David could say with such assurance, "I shall lack nothing. There isn't a thing in the world I need that he doesn't supply."

He makes me lie down in green pastures,
he leads me beside quiet waters.

Can you picture a more peaceful scene? A clear, sparkling brook winds its way through the greenest of pastures. This is no turbulent stream angrily finding its course through a parched, rock-strewn land, void of any living thing, but instead one of the most tranquil spots one can imagine for feeding, watering, and resting. And he provides it for me!

He restores my soul.
He guides me in paths of righteousness
for his name's sake.

Yes, my Shepherd knows that I become discouraged, that doubts and fears can overwhelm me. But he says he will not leave me there. Instead he promises to restore my soul to where he wants it, to where it should be. And then he shows me, not just for my sake but for his as well, the path I should travel and the direction my life should take.

Even though I walk
through the valley of the shadow of death,

I will fear no evil,
    for you are with me;
your rod and your staff,
    they comfort me.

How wonderful to know that God goes with me every-place, even in the shadow of death, whether it be my own death or that of a loved one. I need fear nothing, for my Shepherd's rod and staff are there to help me. True, both may be used for punishment, but even when God has to correct and chastise me he promises that I will be comforted . . . that the final result will be for my good.

You prepare a table before me
    in the presence of my enemies
You anoint my head with oil;
    my cup overflows.

To set a table with all kinds of delicious food and then invite me to partake shows a real love and concern for me. But even more remarkable is that I am invited to do so in the presence of my enemies. God will not allow harm to come to me, but he will guard me and keep my enemies from harming me as I feast at his table. Then he anoints my head with oil—a sign of God's favor and of his healing. He also provides a cup running over—not only full, but with so many blessings that I cannot hold them all! What more could I want?

Surely goodness and love will follow me
    all the days of my life,
And I will dwell in the house of the
    LORD forever.

Thank you, Lord, for this promise and for the assurance that your goodness and love will be with me as long as I live. And then to think that I shall be with my Lord forever—in this life, yes, but also in the life to come, always dwelling with my Lord. What a wonderful future awaits me . . . awaits all of us who are Christians!

Thank you, God, for the beautiful twenty-third psalm. May its reminders comfort me and its promises fill me with thanksgiving. May I repeat it often and may it help make me thankful, happy, and serene. In your name, Amen.

X Games

Action Sports Grab the Spotlight

by Ian Young

Reading Consultant:
Timothy Rasinski, Ph.D.
Professor of Reading Education
Kent State University

Content Consultant:
Patrice Quintero
USA Cycling

Red Brick™ Learning

Published by Red Brick™ Learning
7825 Telegraph Road, Bloomington, Minnesota 55438
http://www.redbricklearning.com

Library of Congress Cataloging-in-Publication Data
Young, Ian, 1970–
    X Games: action sports grab the spotlight/by Ian Young; reading consultant,
Timothy Rasinski.
        p. cm.—(High five reading)
        Includes bibliographical references (p. 46) and index.
        Summary: Examines the showcase for today's action sports, the X Games;
also looks at the rise in popularity of action sports, the birth and growth of the
X Games, the various competitions at the Summer and Winter X Games, and
many of the tricks and moves that action athletes perform.
        ISBN 0-7368-9524-8 (pbk.) - ISBN 0-7368-9546-9 (hardcover)
        1. ESPN X-Games—Juvenile literature. 2. Extreme sports—Juvenile
literature. I. Rasinski, Timothy. II. Title III. Series.
GV722.5.E76 Y68 2002
796—dc21
                                    2002000186

Created by Kent Publishing Services, Inc.
Executive Editor: Robbie Butler
Designed by Signature Design Group, Inc.

Photo Credits:
Cover, Dumo/Corbis; pages 7, 9, 17, UPI/NewsCom; page 10, Michael
Kleinfeld/UPI Photo Service; page 13, UPI Photo/NewsCom; pages 15, 41,
Chris McGrath/Allsport; pages 18, 43, Duomo/Corbis; pages 20, 39, Jon Adams,
UPI Photo Service; pages 23, 31, 33, NewsCom; page 26, Al Bello/Allsport;
page 28, Michael Wong/Corbis; pages 29, Zuma Press; page 34, Martin Philbey,
Zuma Press; page 42, Todd Gipstein/Corbis

Printed in the United States of America.

2 3 4 5 6 08 07 06 05

Table of Contents

Chapter 1

Action Sports Are Born

Have you ever skated a halfpipe? Dirt jumped a BMX? Caught air on a snowboard or wakeboard? Do you like sports with lots of action? If so, the X Games are for you.

4

Not Just for Kids Anymore

Bikes and boards are loads of fun. But in the past kids put the skateboard or the BMX away in high school. School sports like football, soccer, and baseball took over.

Times have changed. Bikes and boards are big today. The people who ride them are now trained **athletes**. They work hard at their sports. And they are not just kids.

These sports are thrilling and daring. Athletes often take risks when they perform. Falls and crashes happen a lot. But high risk is part of these sports. That's one reason they are called "**extreme**" sports.

Andy McDonald skates the halfpipe during the 2001 Summer X Games.

athlete: a person trained in a sport
extreme: very great; the farthest out

From the Sidewalk to the Stadium

The first **official** extreme sport **competition** took place in 1995. It was called the *Extreme Games*. The event was a big success. So the **organizers** held it again the next year. But they gave it a new name—the *Summer X Games*. They had shortened the word *extreme* to *X*.

The Summer X Games take place every year now. Many call the games the "Olympics for young people." More than 250,000 fans went to the Summer X Games in Philadelphia in August 2001.

More new fans attend the X Games each year. Some **marvel** at the speed and danger of street luge racing. Others cheer the stunts of skateboarders and BMX riders. The X Games are a fun, thrilling event.

---

stadium: a building where sports and other events are held
official: approved by someone in authority
competition: a contest
organizer: a person who puts on an event
marvel: to be surprised and amazed

Summer X Games Events

Inline Skating
Park
Vert

BMX
Downhill
Park Riding
Dirt Jump
Vert
Flatland

Skateboarding
Street
Park
Vert
Vert Best Trick
Vert Doubles
Super Mass
King of the Hill

Street Luge
(single event)

Speed Climbing
(single event)

Wakeboarding
(single event)

Moto X
Freestyle
Step Up

Alan Cooke gets "big air."

The Winter X Games

Extreme sports take place in winter, too. The first-ever Winter X Games took place in January 1997. More than 40,000 fans came to Big Bear Lake, California, to watch. Athletes competed at snowboarding, ice climbing, snow BMX, and Moto X racing. There was even a shovel-racing event!

The Winter X Games are now held each year. The four-day contest brings more than 350 competitors and 80,000 fans together. They come from all over the world!

Every year the Winter and Summer X Games grow larger. Why do you think more and more fans are coming?

Winter X Games Events

Skiing
Big Air
Skier X

Snocross
(single event)

Hillcross
(single event)

Snowboarding
Big Air
Slopestyle
Superpipe
Snowboarder X

Ultracross
(single event)

Moto X Big Air
(single event)

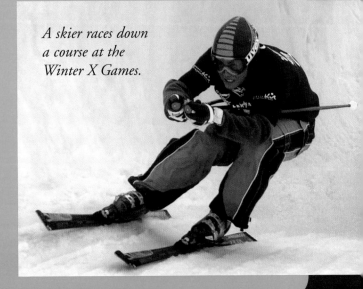

A skier races down a course at the Winter X Games.

— CHAPTER **2** —

Obstacle Xcitement

Ever tried a frontside grind down a handrail? Or a 50-50 railslide off a picnic table in the snow? The Park and Slopestyle events let X Games athletes show off their extreme skills.

Eric Koston does a trick in the Summer X Games Park skateboarding finals.

Skateboarding Park

In the Summer X Games, "Park" is an **obstacle** course. The course is like a public park. There are parking **barriers**, stairs, handrails, and **ramps**. Skaters jump barriers and grind (slide) down rails.

The Park skateboarding event has 20 skaters. Each athlete makes two **runs**. But they don't race against time. The winner is the skater who the judges think had the best runs.

Skateboarders spend years learning new tricks and moves. Each move has its own name. Some moves are named after the first skater to try them. "Ollie" and "Caballerial" are two examples.

---

obstacle: something that blocks or stands in the way
barrier: a fence, wall, or other object that blocks the way
ramp: a sloping surface that links one level with another
run: a race down a course

Inline Skating Park

The Summer X Games also have a Park competition for inline skaters. Inline skaters do tricks like the skateboarders. They jump stairs and grind down handrails. This skating is called "**aggressive** inline skating."

The aggressive skaters compete on the same course as the skateboarders. They also have two runs to show the judges their skills.

Most skaters plan their runs in advance. American skater Jaren Grob did this at the 2001 X Games. He followed his plan for the first run. But he didn't skate well. For his last run he made no plans. He counted on his **instincts** and skill. Guess what? He won the gold medal.

---

aggressive: bold and active
instinct: a way of acting that is natural rather than learned

Jaren Grob shows his skill at aggressive inline skating.

Snowboarding Slopestyle

Slopestyle is the Winter X Games' **version** of Park. It is a snowboard contest. The athletes complete an obstacle course run down a mountain!

The obstacles are called "hits." They include things such as a picnic table and a mailbox. The Slopestyle run also has snow-covered stairs, ramps, and rails.

Like skaters, snowboarders learn a lot of tricks. The tricks have names like "50-50 Railslide" and "Backside 540." In the 50-50 Railslide, the snowboarder ollies (jumps) onto a rail and slides down.

The best Slopestyle and Park athletes are **creative**. They use obstacles to **launch** into tricks. The crowd never knows what these racers will do next!

---

version: a different or changed form of something
creative: using imagination
launch: to start something

This snowboarder grinds down a rail with style.

15

Park Takes to the Water

Imagine snowboarding on water. That's what wakeboarding is like. Athletes jump and spin off a speedboat's **wake**. Wakeboarding is the fastest growing water sport in America.

For the 2001 Summer X Games, there was a wakeboarding obstacle course. The obstacles had names like "Slaughter Box," "Kicker," and "Slider." Athletes had to jump the obstacles or slide across them. **Competitors** thrilled the crowd with air spins, jumps, and flips.

American stars Darin Shapiro and Erik Ruck invented two new tricks at the 2001 Games. This often happens in the X Games. The games push the athletes to new levels of skill.

---

wake: waves in water made by a boat
competitor: a person who takes part in a contest

The event was a huge success. Two teens even won gold medals. The men's winner, Danny Harf, was just 16. The women's winner, Dallas Friday, was only 14!

In some extreme sports speed is as important as skill. Learn more about these sports in the next chapter.

Trevor Hansen shows the excitement of wakeboarding.

CHAPTER 3

Speed Kings

*Some X Games events are battles of speed.
To win, you must cross the finish line first.
Athletes race on BMX, snowmobiles, and
street luges. Let the races begin!*

*Imagine soaring down a street with no brakes
like these Street Luge riders.*

Street Luge

Street Luge is one of the most thrilling contests in the Summer X Games. The downhill course is a closed public road. Hay **bales** line the road for safety.

The luge is made from wood, steel, or **aluminum**. The luge has no brakes or steering wheel. The riders lean their bodies into turns to steer. They press their shoes on the ground to brake. Riders can reach speeds of more than 70 miles (113 kilometers) per hour.

Fans enjoy two Street Luge events. The first is called "Super Mass." The winner from each Super Mass **heat** goes to the next round. There are four heats to decide who reaches the final.

After the finals of the Super Mass, the new winner races against winners from past years. The winner of that race is called "King of the Hill."

---

bale: a large bundle, usually of dried grass
aluminum: a lightweight metal
heat: a round or stage of an event

Downhill BMX

There are many tough obstacles on the Downhill BMX course. Forty-foot (12.2-meter) jumps, giant tabletops, and an 8-foot (2.4-meter) drop are among the tests. Riders begin the race at the same time. The winner is the first to complete the course.

The Summer X Games **staged** the Downhill BMX for the first time in 2001. Thousands of fans came to watch. They wanted to see a thrilling race. They were not let down.

---

stage: to hold

All 30 riders **swarmed** over the course like bees. Some riders passed others on the jumps. Imagine passing another biker while in the air!

A young American rider, Brandon Meadows, won the race. But it was very close. Leader Robbie Miranda crashed on the final jump and was knocked **unconscious**. He was okay later. His safety gear protected him.

---

swarm: to move together in a thick mass
unconscious: not awake; not able to see, feel, or think

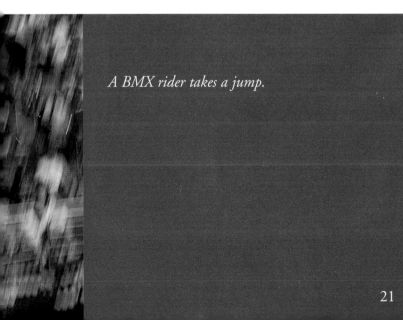

A BMX rider takes a jump.

SnoCross and HillCross

People describe SnoCross as **NASCAR** on snow. The racers ride snowmobiles. These snowmobiles are **modified** to go fast. SnoCross drivers can hit speeds of 70 miles (113 kilometers) per hour.

All the racers depend on their **mechanics**. Good mechanics knows how to prepare the snowmobile to make it run its best.

One recent SnoCross star is Tucker Hibbert. Tucker is the son of SnoCross **legend** Kirk Hibbert. Tucker won his first gold medal at age 16. He could not even drive a car at that time! Tucker and Kirk are the first father and son to compete in the same X Games.

NASCAR: National Association for Stock Car Auto Racing
modify: to change slightly
mechanic: a person who builds and repairs machinery
legend: a person who is much talked about

The HillCross event was held for the first time in 2001. HillCross is like SnoCross. But there is one big difference. HillCross is run uphill. Imagine 18 snowmobiles roaring up a mountain! Racers compete for the title "King of the Hill," just like in Street Luge.

Nathan Zollinger speeds up the slopes during the Hillcross event at the 2001 Winter X Games at Mount Snow.

Speed Climbing

Speed climbing differs from mountain climbing. The **challenge** is not just to reach the top. It's to reach the top before anyone else.

Speed climbing takes place on man-made walls. The walls are dotted with different grips or handles. These grips have names like "jug," "crimper," or "pocket." The climber must use the grips to **scale** the wall.

In the X Games, climbers go "head-to-head." Two **contestants** race to the top. Whoever hits the buzzer at the top first is the winner. This competition lasts until only two climbers remain. The final pair then races to decide the winner. Sometimes the race is won by less than one second.

---

challenge: a test or obstacle to be overcome
scale: to climb
contestant: a person who plays in a game or sports competition

The best speed climbers in the world today are European and Asian. Both male and female 2001 X Games winners were from the Ukraine in eastern Europe. In fact, the top three women came from the same town.

Safety is important in speed climbing. Climbers are tied to a safety rope. It doesn't help them climb, but it stops them if they fall.

Ready for more thrills? Read the next chapter to find out about extreme stunts in the air.

Elena Repko, 2001 speed climbing champion

— CHAPTER **4** —

Skill in the Air

How high can you jump? How many spins can you do during a flip? The more "air" you can find, the bigger the trick! Welcome to the world of the dirt jump and the halfpipe.

Ross Powers competes in the Superpipe snowboard event at the 2002 Winter X Games.

Big Air in the Snow

In the Winter X Games, snowboarders and skiers compete in Big Air contests. The athletes blast down a hill and leap off a ramp. Then they try to go as "big" or as high as they can. Jumpers do twists, spins, and even back flips. Whatever they do, they must impress the judges. "Sticking the landing" or staying upright is also very important to winning.

The **acrobatics** of Big Air are fun to watch. Each competitor has three tries to do his or her best trick. The **tension** builds as each jumper runs out of chances. Sometimes the gold medal is won on the last try!

---

acrobatics: stunts and tricks
tension: excitement

Big Air on Bikes

Summer X Games fans enjoy the BMX Dirt Jump and Moto X (motocross) Big Air. These races have a fun feeling. The place rocks with music and cheering.

The BMX Dirt Jump is a man-made mound of dirt. The mound takes 300 truckloads of dirt to build. Riders jump the mound and perform a trick.

These tricks also have special names such as "Tailwhip," "Truckdriver," and "Superman." The double back flip is the hardest. American Stephen Murray landed one in the 2001 X Games. He also landed the gold medal.

Big air on a BMX

The Moto X Big Air event rocks, too. Like BMX Dirt Jump, the Moto X Big Air is a single trick event. But there is a difference— the smell. The air at Moto X is thick with oil and **exhaust fumes**.

The Moto X riders perform daring stunts. Picture someone trying to do a back flip on a motorbike. American Carey Hart was the first to do it. But at the 2001 X Games, Hart fell when he landed. He was taken to the hospital with two broken ribs.

A Moto X Superman seat grab

---

exhaust fumes: waste gases produced by an engine

The Challenge of Vert

Fans all over the world know the Vert ramp. It is a **symbol** of the X Games. The Vert ramp is best known in skateboarding contests. But BMX bikers, inline skaters, and snowboarders also have Vert contests.

The Vert ramp looks like a pipe cut in half. That's why it is called the "halfpipe." *Vert* describes a halfpipe that goes several feet straight up—or **vertical**—at the top. In the 2001 X Games, the Vert ramp was more than 12 feet (3.7 meters) high and 56 feet (17 meters) wide.

In a Vert ramp, athletes skate or ride from edge to edge. They gain speed until they soar into the air and do a trick. Athletes and fans get "stoked" or excited when someone lands a big trick.

---

symbol: an object that stands for something else
vertical: straight up

One very popular Vert event is the doubles. In this event, two skateboarders ride side-by-side and do tricks at the same time. They perform airs (jumps) together. Sometimes they even switch boards.

Flips and twists are common in skateboarding. But there is one trick only the best skateboarder can do—the "900."

The Vert doubles

Tony Hawk and the "900"

Skateboarder Tony Hawk is the most famous Vert athlete. He landed the first 900. This is a two-and-a-half-turn spin in the air. It is one of the hardest tricks in skateboarding. This trick made Hawk the first X Games superstar.

Hawk had been trying to do the 900 for more than 10 years. Every time he failed, he hurt himself. So he couldn't try too often!

He finally landed the 900 at the 1999 X Games. The event made the national news. Hawk became even more famous. The X Games also became major news. A whole new sporting **culture** had arrived.

Would you be stoked to compete in the X Games? Read on to learn more about this exciting sport.

---

culture: a way of life; custom

Tony Hawk attempts the 900.

CHAPTER 5

The X Games Worldwide

The X Games get bigger every year. Events take place all over the world. There are X Game movies and tours. The X Games are now a major sports event.

*Extreme bikers **demonstrate** their sport at the 2000 Summer X Games in Australia.*

How to Qualify

The level of skill in the X Games is very high. Athletes must first **qualify** to compete. To qualify, athletes must take part in an X Games Qualifier.

There are four events where athletes can qualify. They take place in four different countries. Each event hosts the best athletes in a **region**. The winners then compete in the X Games in the United States.

The X Games Qualifiers often find new talent. There are great skaters in countries like Malaysia and Brazil. Ukraine, in eastern Europe, produces great climbers. New stars help the games grow.

The X Games also include young athletes. A Junior X Games event is held with each qualifying event. These are for athletes aged 14 and under. Junior X Games are a great way for kids to learn.

---

demonstrate: to show other people how to do something
qualify: to reach a level that allows you to do something
region: a distinct area of land

Ultimate X: the Movie

Action sports look awesome on the movie screen. The Disney Company made a film about the X Games. *Ultimate X* came out in 2002. It was filmed at the 2001 Summer X Games in Philadelphia.

The movie is shown in giant-screen IMAX theaters. The screens in these theaters are six stories high and eight stories wide! The **audience** feels like they are in the middle of the action.

The film crew for *Ultimate X* followed all the sports. They used special cameras to get great shots. They tried to show tricks and stunts the way a rider sees them.

---

audience: people who gather to hear or watch something

Ultimate X shows more than great tricks, though. The movie also shows the friendly, helpful feeling many X Games athletes share.

Bruce Hendricks **directed** *Ultimate X*. He remembers seeing something that showed this special feeling.

"Motocross star Carey Hart was training," Hendricks said. "So here's this motocross star and one of his friends rides BMX. And there was an inline skater hanging out with them. They were helping each other with training **techniques** and stuff like that."

---

direct: to be in charge of
technique: a way of doing something

X Games on Tour

The X Games have many fans. To support these fans, X Games stars go on **tours**. The stars pile into a big bus and visit as many places as they can.

Tour events are free to the public. Athletes meet and talk with their fans. They share advice and give **autographs**. They even hold fun competitions to find the best local talent. Who knows? They might even find a new X Games star.

Skateboarder Tony Hawk launched the Gigantic Skatepark Tour in 2000. Hawk took a group of skateboarders and BMX riders. They visited more than a dozen skateparks in the United States. At each stop they put on shows. Hawk even took his Gigantic Tour to Europe.

---

tour: a trip to different places to perform
autograph: a person's handwritten name

Tony Hawk soars on the skateboard.

Epilogue

The world of action sports has many of its own words and phrases. Most describe a trick. Some, such as *stoked*, tell about feelings. Here is a sample of some common words. The key shows which sports the word or phrase is used in.

KEY

SKT—Skateboarding   INL—Inline skating

SNB—Snowboarding   MTX—Motocross

BMX—BMX biking   MULTI—Several or all action sports

Abadaca (BMX): ride up the ramp, touch the back tire on the top edge of the ramp, and go back down backward

Air (MULTI): any trick done in the air

Air to fakie (SNB): approach the ramp forward, do an air trick, then land backward

Alley-oop (SKT): do a trick in the opposite direction to which you are moving

Backside air (SNB): any air done on the back wall of the halfpipe

Bar spin (BMX): spin handlebars during an air and grab them before landing

Bio grab (INL): grab the outside of the skate with the hand of the same side

Board (SKT): also called a "deck," the platform you ride on

Boardslide/Railslide (SKT): slide on an obstacle or edge using the bottom of the board

Butter slide (MULTI): slide on wake or snow with board facing sideways to direction of travel

Camel (INL): tap the toe during re-entry onto a ramp or obstacle

Canyon (BMX): space between dirt ramps or ramps on a street course

Carve (SKT): make a long, curving arc while skating

Cased (MULTI): land short or miss a landing

Cliffhanger (MTX): hook feet under the bars and raise hands in the air

Coping (MULTI): rounded edge at top of ramp or obstacle

Disaster (SNB): get stuck on the coping

Double grab (SNB): doing two separate tricks while in the air

Drop in (MULTI): enter a ramp or obstacle from the top

Fakie (MULTI): ride backward

Flatland (MULTI): tricks on level ground using obstacles

Freeriding (SNB): snowboarding on all types of surfaces for fun

Fun box (BMX): box with a ramp on every side

Grind plate (INL): plastic or metal piece attached to the frame of the skate; used to slide on

Halfpipe (MULTI): ramp that is U-shaped and used for Vert

Hand plant (MULTI): trick where a one-handed handstand is done off an obstacle. The other hand holds the skate.

Hang up (INL): catch one or both skates on the edge of a ramp or obstacle during re-entry

Heelflip (SKT): during an Ollie, the heel pushes down on the edge of the board, causing it to flip over

Hip (MULTI): where a ramp or obstacle comes to a point

Ho ho (MULTI): any two-handed hand plant

Hucker (SNB): throw yourself wildly through the air and not land on your feet

Invert (MULTI): another word for a hand plant

Kickflip (SKT): like a heelflip, except the toe pushes down on the board

Kick turn (SKT): press down on the tail of the board, lift the front, and turn it in another direction

Knee slide (MULTI): controlling a fall by sliding on the kneepads

Look back (BMX): a rider in the air turns the handlebars and body backward

Nac nac (MTX): a rider pretends to get off in mid-air

No hander lander (MTX): landing a jump with no hands on the bars

Nollie (MULTI): like an Ollie, only you spring off the nose instead of the tail

Ollie (MULTI): no-handed air done by tapping the tail of the board on the ground or ramp surface

Revert (SNB): switch from fakie to forward, or from forward to fakie

Rocket air (INL): grab both skates with your hands while your feet are stretched out in front

Rolling down the windows (SNB): when someone is off balance and rotates the arms wildly to try and recover

Run (MULTI): set series of tricks

Session (MULTI): period of skating or riding

Shovel (SNB): lifted or curved sections of the snowboard at the tip and tail

Stall (BMX): where the rider pauses briefly on the coping before dropping back into the ramp

Superman (BMX): rider stretches legs as far back as possible to look like Superman flying on the handlebars

Tabletop (MULTI): type of jump with a ramp going up, a flat top, and a landing ramp on the other side

Truck (SKT): hardware (axle and base plate) fixed to the board

Turndown (BMX): turn the handlebars and the body down toward the ground while the rest of the bike stays facing up

Tweaked (SNB): style in a trick

Varial (SKT): aerial trick where the board is spun from backward to forward beneath the feet

Variation (MULTI): to change from one type of grab or hold to another during a long trick such as a handrail

Vert (MULTI): short for "vertical," meaning a 90-degree ramp or wall. Also refers to the halfpipe event.

Wall (MULTI): any bank that is at or above 90 degrees

Glossary

acrobatics: stunts and tricks

aggressive: bold and active

aluminum: a lightweight metal

athlete: a person trained in a sport

audience: people who gather to hear or watch something

autograph: a person's handwritten name

bale: a large bundle, usually of dried grass

barrier: a fence, wall, or other object that blocks the way

challenge: a test or obstacle to be overcome

competition: a contest

competitor: a person who takes part in a contest

contestant: a person who plays in a game or
    sports competition

creative: using imagination

culture: a way of life; custom

demonstrate: to show other people how to do something

direct: to be in charge of

exhaust fumes: waste gases produced by an engine

extreme: very great; the farthest out

heat: a round or stage of an event

instinct: a way of acting that is natural rather than learned

launch: to start something

legend: a person who is much talked about

marvel: to be surprised and amazed
mechanic: a person who builds and repairs machinery
modify: to change slightly
NASCAR: National Association for Stock Car Auto Racing
obstacle: something that blocks or stands in the way
official: approved by someone in authority
organizer: a person who puts on an event
qualify: to reach a level that allows you to do something
ramp: a sloping surface that links one level with another
region: a distinct area of land
run: a race down a course
scale: to climb
stadium: a building where sports and other events are held
stage: to hold
swarm: to move together in a thick mass
symbol: an object that stands for something else
technique: a way of doing something
tension: excitement
tour: a trip to different places to perform
unconscious: not awake; not able to see, feel, or think
version: a different or changed form of something
vertical: straight up
wake: waves in water made by a boat

Bibliography

Blomquist, Christopher. *Motocross in the X Games*. Kid's Guide to the X Games. New York: PowerKids Press, 2003.

Hoffman, Matt. *Brady Games: Matt Hoffman's Pro BMX Official Strategy*. New York: Pearson Professional Education, 2001.

McKenna, Anne T. *Extreme Wakeboarding*, Extreme Sports. Mankato, Minn.: Capstone Press, 1999.

Ryan, Kevin. *The Illustrated Guide to Snowboarding*. Indianapolis, Ind.: Masters Press, 1998.

Ryan, Pat. *Street Luge Racing*. Extreme Sports. Mankato, Minn.: Capstone Press, 1998.

Stout, Glen. *On the Halfpipe with Tony Hawk*. Boston: Little Brown, and Company, 2001.

Useful Addresses

Canadian Snowcross Racing Association
P.O. Box 51
Keswick, Ontario L4P 3E1
Canada

Internet Sites

CSRA/ASRA (SnoCross)
www.snowcross.com

EXPN
www.expn.com

Inline Skating Resource Center
www.iisa.org

MXmotocross.com
www.motocross.com

Skateboard Science
www.exploratorium.edu/
skateboarding/

World Wakeboarding Association
www.thewwa.com

Index